ITALIAN COOKBOOK

1000 DAYS SIMPLE AND EASY AUTHENTIC ITALIAN RECIPES ENJOYING IN YOUR OWN HOME

By Megha Sehgal

© Copyright 2023 - All rights reserved.

In no way is it legal to reproduce, duplicate, or transmit any part of this document in either electronic means or in printed format. Recording of this publication is strictly prohibited and any storage of this document is not allowed unless with written permission from the publisher. All rights reserved.

The information provided herein is stated to be truthful and consistent, in that any liability, in terms of inattention or otherwise, by any usage or abuse of any policies, processes, or directions contained within is the solitary and utter responsibility of the recipient reader.

Under no circumstances will any legal responsibility or blame be held against the publisher for any reparation, damages, or monetary loss due to the information herein, either directly or indirectly. Respective authors own all copyrights not held by the publisher.

Legal Notice:

This book is copyright protected. This is only for personal use. You cannot amend, distribute, sell, use, quote or paraphrase any part or the content within this book without the consent of the author or copyright owner. Legal action will be pursued if this is breached.

Published by Megha Sehgal

TABLE OF CONTENTS

Introduction 7
Italian cooking history 7
Italian flavors 8
APPETIZERS 9

- Arancini Sicilian Rice Balls 9
- Calamari Fritti Fried Calamari 9
- Impepata di Cozze Peppered Mussels 10
- Carciofi alla Giudea Roman-Style Fried Artichokes 10
- Panelle Sicilian Chickpea Fritters 11
- Polenta e Gamberett Salad Shrimp over Creamy Polenta 11
- Capesante Gratinate alla Veneziana Venetian-Style Baked Sea Scallops 12
- Traditional Bruschetta with Fresh Tomatoes 13
- Crostini with Prosciutto and Burrata 13
- Mozzarelle in Carrozza Venetian Fried Mozzarella Sandwiches 14
- Frittata alle Cipolle Onion Frittata 14
- Frittata di Spaghetti Neapolitan Spaghetti Frittata 15

SOUPS AND SALADS 16

- Pasta e Fagioli alla Veneta Venetian-Style Beans and Pasta Soup 16
- Minestrone Soup 16
- Pasta e Ceci Chickpeas and Pasta Soup 17
- Ribollita Tuscan Kale and Bread Soup 17
- Passatelli in Brodo Homemade Passatelli Pasta in Broth from Emilia 18
- Zuppa d'Orzo Barley Soup from Alto Adige 19
- Caprese Salad 19
- Radicchio, Arugula, and Shaved Fennel Salad with Anchovy 20
- Vinaigrette 20
- Caponata di Tonno Neapolitan Tuna, Tomato, and Bread Salad 20
- Insalata di Finocchi e Arance Sicilian Fennel and Orange Salad 21
- Panzanella Tuscan Bread and Tomato Salad 22
- Farro Salad 22

RISOTTO AND POLENTA 24

- Risotto alla Milanese Risotto with Saffron 24
- Risotto with Porcini Mushrooms 24

Risotto with Radicchio and Sausage 25
Risotto allo Scoglio Seafood Risotto 26
Risotto al Salto Crispy Rice Cake 26
Risotto with Shrimp and Asparagus 27
Risi e Bisi Veneto-Style Rice and Peas 28
Basic Polenta 28
Grilled Polenta 29
Baked Polenta with Cheese, Mushrooms, and Sausage 29

SAUCES AND PASTA 31

Basic Tomato Sauce 31
Ravi alla Bolognese Meat Sauce 31
Pesto alla Genovese Pesto Sauce 32
Besciamella Sauce White Sauce 32
Homemade Egg Tagliatelle Pasta 33
Homemade Spinach Ricotta Ravioli 33
Spaghetti alla Carbonara 34
Pasta all'Amatriciana 34
Cacio e Pepe Cheese and Pepper Pasta 35
Penne alla Vodka Penne Pasta with Vodka Sauce 35
Spaghetti alle Vongole Spaghetti with Clam Sauce 36
Spaghetti Aglio Olio e Peperoncino Spaghetti with Garlic, Oil, and Hot Peppers 37
Troli e alla Genovese Pasta with Pesto, Green Beans, and Potatoes 37
Traditional Lasagna 38
Pasta alla Norma Sicilian Pasta with Eggplant Sauce 38
Potato Gnocchi 39
Gnocchi alla Sorrentina 40
Bigoi in Salsa Pasta with Anchovy Sauce, Venetian Style 40

PIZZA AND BREAD 42

Homemade Pizza Dough 42
Pizza Margherita 42
Pizza with Burrata Cheese and Fresh Tomatoes 43
Panzerotti Fried Stuffed Pizza 43
Gnocco Fritto Fried Homemade Bread 44
Rosemary Focaccia Bread 44
Focaccia Bread with Cherry Tomatoes 45
Garlic Rolls 46
Ciabatta Bread 46
Pane Rustico Pugliese Rustic Bread Loaf 47

MEAT AND POULTRY 47

Saltimbocca alla Romana Roman-Style Veal Scaloppine 47
Ossobuchi alla Milanese Milanese-Style Veal Shank 48

Pollo alla Cacciatora Hunter's Chicken Stew ... 49
Polpette al Sugo Meatballs in Tomato Sauce ... 49
Polpette Fritte Fried Meatballs ... 50
Cotoletta alla Milanese Milanese-Style Veal Chop ... 51
Brasato al Barolo Beef Stew Braised in Barolo Wine ... 51
Scaloppine al Marsala con Funghi Marsala Scaloppine with Mushrooms ... 52
Cosce d'Anatra Brasate Braised Duck Legs ... 52
Scottadito alla Romana Roman-Style Grilled Lamb Chops ... 53
Brasato di Maiale alla Birra Beer-Braised Pork Stew ... 53
Spezzattino di Pollo all'Arrabbiata Chicken Stew all'Arrabbiata ... 54

FISH AND SEAFOOD ... 56

Insalata di Polpo e Patate Octopus and Potato Salad ... 56
Polpo alla Griglia Grilled Octopus with Vegetables ... 56
Calamari Ripieni Stuffed Calamari ... 57
Cozze Gratinate Pugliesi Baked Stuffed Mussels ... 57
Sogliola alla Mugnaia Sautéed Dover Sole with Lemon ... 58
Zuppa di Pesce Fish Stew ... 58
Pesce Spada alla Siciliana Sicilian-Style Swordfish ... 59
Filetti di Dentice al Cartoccio Red Snapper Fillets Baked in Foil ... 60
Filetti di Branzino alla Genovese Genoa-Style Branzino with Potatoes and Olives ... 60
Polpette al Tonno Tuna Meatballs ... 61
Salmone con Finocchio Baked Salmon Fillets with Shaved Fennel ... 61
Gamberoni alla Busara Venetian-Style Prawns in Tomato Sauce ... 62

VEGETABLES ... 63

Parmigiana di Melanzane Eggplant Parmigiana ... 63
Caponata di Melanzane Sicilian Eggplant Stew ... 63
Pomodori Gratinati Baked Tomato Gratin ... 64
Pomodori Ripieni Tomatoes Stuffed with Rice ... 64
Peperonata Sauteed Peppers ... 65
Fagiolini alla Genovese Genoa-Style Green Beans ... 65
Carcioli alla Romana Roman-Style Artichokes ... 66
Insalata Calabrese di Patate Calabrian-Style Potato Salad ... 66
Patate Arroste Roasted Potatoes ... 67
Pasticcio di Patate con Funghi Potato Lasagna with Mushrooms ... 67

DESSERTS AND DRINKS ... 69

Tiramisii ... 69
Panna Cotta with Berry Sauce ... 69
Cantucci Biscotti ... 70
Pasticcini alle Mandorle Almond Cookies ... 70
Zeppole alla Ricotta Ricotta Fritters ... 71
Torta della Nonna Grandma's Cake ... 72

Baci di Dama Chocolate and Hazelnut Sandwich Cookies 72
Migliaccio Neapolitan Ricotta Cake 73
Roman Maritozzi alla Panna 73
Cannoncini alla Crema Cream-Stuffed Horns 74
Spritz Cocktail 74
Bellini Cocktail 75
Mimosa Cocktail 75
Sgroppino Cocktail 76

Conclusion 77

INTRODUCTION

Welcome to the wonderful world of Italian cuisine! Italian food is one of the most popular and beloved cuisines around the globe, known for its simple yet delicious flavors, fresh ingredients, and rich history.

Italian cooking has its roots in traditional family recipes passed down through generations, but it has also evolved and adapted to incorporate new techniques and ingredients over time. Some of the most famous Italian dishes include pizza, pasta, risotto, and antipasti, but there is so much more to explore.

In this cookbook, we will explore a wide range of Italian dishes, from classic favorites to modern twists on traditional recipes. You'll learn how to make everything from simple sauces to complex dishes, and we'll also cover tips and tricks for getting the most out of your ingredients and equipment.

So whether you're a seasoned home cook or just starting out, this cookbook is the perfect guide to help you bring the flavors of Italy into your kitchen. Let's get cooking!

ITALIAN COOKING HISTORY

Italian cuisine has a rich and diverse history that dates back to ancient times. The cuisine has been influenced by various factors such as geography, climate, cultural and political changes, as well as trade and colonization. Italian cuisine is the result of a long process of evolution, experimentation, and creativity.

The ancient Romans made significant contributions to Italian cuisine, introducing new ingredients such as garlic, onions, and wine. They also developed various cooking techniques and methods, including the use of ovens, deep frying, and roasting.

During the Middle Ages, Italy experienced a period of cultural, economic, and social growth. The cuisine during this time was simple, yet flavorful, using ingredients such as cheese, bread, and vegetables.

The Renaissance period saw an explosion in Italian cuisine, as wealthy families began to hire professional cooks and chefs to prepare lavish feasts. This period saw the development of new techniques, such as cooking with butter and the use of cream sauces.

In the 18th century, Italy was divided into small states, and each region developed its own unique cuisine, based on the local ingredients and traditions. This led to the development of various regional dishes that are still popular today, such as pizza from Naples and risotto from Milan.

In the 20th century, Italian cuisine began to gain international recognition, thanks in part to the large number of Italian immigrants who brought their recipes and cooking techniques with them to other countries. Today, Italian cuisine is known and loved around the world for its use of fresh, high-quality ingredients, simple yet delicious flavors, and its emphasis on family and tradition.

ITALIAN FLAVORS

Italian cuisine is famous for its delicious and distinctive flavors that come from a combination of fresh, high-quality ingredients and traditional cooking techniques. Some of the most common Italian flavors include:

1. Garlic: Garlic is a staple ingredient in Italian cuisine and is used to add depth and complexity to many dishes, from pasta sauces to stews and soups.
2. Olive oil: Olive oil is a key ingredient in Italian cooking and is used for everything from sautéing vegetables to dressing salads. High-quality extra virgin olive oil is often used to drizzle over finished dishes for added flavor.
3. Tomato: Tomatoes are a staple in Italian cuisine and are used in everything from pasta sauces to soups and stews. Fresh, ripe tomatoes are preferred, but canned tomatoes are also commonly used.
4. Basil: Fresh basil is a common herb used in Italian cuisine and is used to add a bright, fresh flavor to dishes such as pasta, pizza, and bruschetta.
5. Parmesan cheese: Parmesan cheese is a hard, salty cheese that is commonly grated and used to add flavor to pasta dishes, salads, and more.
6. Balsamic vinegar: Balsamic vinegar is a sweet, tangy vinegar that is commonly used as a dressing for salads and as a glaze for meats and vegetables.
7. Oregano: Oregano is a common herb used in Italian cuisine, and is often used to flavor tomato-based sauces, as well as meats and vegetables.
8. Prosciutto: Prosciutto is a type of cured meat that is commonly used in Italian cuisine, and is often served as an antipasto or used to flavor pasta dishes.

Overall, Italian flavors are characterized by their simplicity, freshness, and high-quality ingredients. The focus is on letting the natural flavors of the ingredients shine through, rather than masking them with heavy sauces or seasonings.

APPETIZERS

ARANCINI SICILIAN RICE BALLS

Cook time: 30 minutes
Serving: 8 pieces
Ingredients:
- 2 cups of Arborio Rice
- 4 cups of chicken broth
- 1/2 cup of grated Parmesan cheese
- 1/2 cup of diced onion
- 2 tablespoons of olive oil
- 1 egg
- 1/2 cup of breadcrumbs
- 1/2 cup of marinara sauce
- 1/2 cup of mozzarella cheese
- Salt and pepper to taste
- Vegetable oil for frying

Preparation:
1. In a large saucepan, heat the olive oil and add the diced onion. Cook until translucent.
2. Add the Arborio Rice and stir for 2-3 minutes.
3. Gradually add the chicken broth and stir continuously until the liquid is absorbed.
4. Add the grated Parmesan cheese, salt, and pepper to taste. Mix well.
5. Remove from heat and allow the mixture to cool.
6. Once cooled, form 2 inch diameter balls with the mixture.
7. Using your thumb, create a hole in the center of each ball.
8. Fill the hole with a small amount of marinara sauce and mozzarella cheese.
9. Close the hole by molding the mixture back over the filling.
10. Beat the egg in a bowl.
11. Dip each ball into the beaten egg and then coat with breadcrumbs.
12. In a large saucepan, heat the vegetable oil to 375°F.
13. Fry the rice balls for 5-7 minutes until golden brown.

Serve hot with marinara sauce for dipping.
Nutrition: Per serving (1 rice ball): Calories: 190 Fat: 11g Carbohydrates: 16g Protein: 7g Sodium: 300mg

CALAMARI FRITTI FRIED CALAMARI

Cook time: 15 minutes
Serving: 4
Ingredients:
- 1 lb. calamari tubes and tentacles, cleaned and sliced into rings
- 1 cup all-purpose flour
- 1 tsp. garlic powder
- 1 tsp. paprika
- Salt and pepper to taste
- 2 eggs, beaten
- 1 cup breadcrumbs
- Oil for frying

Preparation:
1. In a shallow dish, mix together the flour, garlic powder, paprika, salt and pepper.
2. In another shallow dish, beat the eggs.
3. In a third shallow dish, place the breadcrumbs.
4. Dip each calamari ring into the flour mixture, shaking off any excess.
5. Then, dip into the beaten eggs.
6. Finally, coat in the breadcrumbs.
7. Repeat this process for all the calamari rings.
8. In a large frying pan, heat the oil over medium-high heat.
9. Once the oil is hot, add the coated calamari rings to the pan. Fry until golden brown on both sides, about 2-3 minutes per side.
10. Remove the calamari fritti from the pan and place on a paper towel to remove any excess oil.
11. Serve hot with your favorite dipping sauce.

Nutrition (per serving): Calories: 380 Fat: 19g Saturated Fat: 2g Cholesterol: 215mg Sodium: 925mg Carbohydrates: 30g Fiber: 2g Sugar: 1g Protein: 22g

IMPEPATA DI COZZE PEPPERED MUSSELS

Cook Time: 20 minutes
Serving: 4
Ingredients:
- 2 pounds mussels, cleaned
- 2 tablespoons olive oil
- 4 garlic cloves, minced
- 1 teaspoon red pepper flakes
- 1 cup dry white wine
- 1 lemon, juiced
- 1 tablespoon chopped fresh parsley
- Salt and pepper, to taste

Preparation:
1. In a large saucepan, heat the olive oil over medium heat. Add the garlic and red pepper flakes and cook until fragrant, about 1 minute.
2. Add the mussels to the pan and cook for 2 minutes, stirring occasionally.
3. Pour in the white wine and lemon juice, and season with salt and pepper. Stir well.
4. Cover the pan with a lid and cook for about 10 minutes, or until the mussels have opened. Discard any mussels that do not open.
5. Stir in the chopped parsley and serve immediately, with crusty bread for dipping in the flavorful broth.

Nutrition: Serving size: 1 cup Calories: 259 Fat: 14g Saturated Fat: 2g Cholesterol: 47mg Sodium: 443mg Carbohydrates: 8g Fiber: 1g Protein: 22g

CARCIOFI ALLA GIUDEA ROMAN-STYLE FRIED ARTICHOKES

Cook time: 20 minutes
Servings: 4
Ingredients:
- 8 medium artichokes
- 2 cups of olive oil for frying

- 1 teaspoon salt
- 1 teaspoon black pepper
- 2 cloves of garlic, minced
- 2 tablespoons lemon juice
- 1 teaspoon dried oregano
- 1 teaspoon dried basil

Preparation:
1. Rinse the artichokes and trim the stems to about 1 inch. Cut off the top third of each artichoke and remove the tough outer leaves.
2. Heat the olive oil in a deep skillet over medium-high heat.
3. Season the artichokes with salt, pepper, garlic, lemon juice, oregano, and basil.
4. Fry the artichokes in the hot oil until they are golden brown, about 8-10 minutes on each side.
5. Remove the artichokes from the oil and drain on paper towels.
6. Serve hot with lemon wedges, if desired.

Nutrition: (per serving) Calories: 441 Total Fat: 43g Saturated Fat: 6gCholesterol: 0mg Sodium: 680mg Total Carbohydrates: 25g Dietary Fiber: 10g Sugar: 4g Protein: 4g.

PANELLE SICILIAN CHICKPEA FRITTERS

Cook Time: 15 minutes
Serving: 4-6
Ingredients:
- 1 1/2 cups chickpea flour
- 1 cup water
- 1/2 teaspoon salt
- 2 tablespoons olive oil
- 2 cloves of garlic, minced
- 1 teaspoon cumin
- 1/2 teaspoon red pepper flakes
- 1 tablespoon parsley, chopped
- Vegetable oil, for frying

Preparation:
1. In a large bowl, whisk together chickpea flour, water, salt, olive oil, garlic, cumin, red pepper flakes, and parsley.
2. Heat a large skillet over medium heat and add enough vegetable oil to shallow fry the fritters.
3. Scoop about 2 tablespoons of the batter into the skillet and flatten it to form a patty. Fry until golden brown, about 2-3 minutes per side.
4. Repeat with remaining batter.
5. Serve hot with a side of lemon wedges and a sprinkle of sea salt.

Nutrition (per serving, based on 6 servings): Calories: 153 Fat: 11g Protein: 5g Carbohydrates: 12g Fiber: 2g Sugar: 1g Sodium: 550mg

POLENTA E GAMBERETT SALAD SHRIMP OVER CREAMY POLENTA

Cook time: 30 minutes
Serving: 4
Ingredients:

- 1 cup polenta
- 4 cups water
- 1/2 cup heavy cream
- 1/2 cup grated parmesan cheese
- Salt and pepper, to taste
- 2 tablespoons olive oil
- 1 pound shrimp, peeled and deveined
- 1 garlic clove, minced
- 1 lemon, juiced
- 2 tablespoons chopped parsley
- 2 tablespoons chopped basil

Preparation:
1. In a large saucepan, bring the water to a boil and add salt to taste. Gradually add the polenta, whisking constantly, until smooth. Reduce heat to low and continue to stir for about 20 minutes or until the mixture becomes thick and creamy.
2. Stir in the heavy cream and grated parmesan cheese until well combined. Season with salt and pepper to taste.
3. In a separate pan, heat the olive oil over medium heat. Add the minced garlic and cook until fragrant, about 1 minute. Add the shrimp and cook for 2-3 minutes on each side or until pink and fully cooked.
4. Remove from heat and squeeze lemon juice over the shrimp. Stir in the chopped parsley and basil.
5. Serve the shrimp over the creamy polenta and garnish with additional chopped herbs, if desired.

Nutrition: Per serving (based on 4 servings): Calories: 455 Fat: 25g Saturated fat: 12g Cholesterol: 269mg Sodium: 796mg Carbohydrates: 28g Fiber: 1g Sugar: 3g Protein: 27g.

CAPESANTE GRATINATE ALLA VENEZIANA VENETIAN-STYLE BAKED SEA SCALLOPS

Cook time: 25 minutes
Serving: 4
Ingredients:
- 16 large sea scallops
- 1 cup breadcrumbs
- 1/4 cup grated Parmesan cheese
- 1/4 cup chopped fresh parsley
- 2 cloves garlic, minced
- Salt and pepper, to taste
- 1/4 cup olive oil

Preparation:
1. Preheat the oven to 400°F (200°C).
2. In a shallow dish, mix together the breadcrumbs, Parmesan cheese, parsley, garlic, salt and pepper.
3. Rinse the scallops and pat dry with paper towels.
4. Dip each scallop into the breadcrumb mixture, making sure they are well coated.
5. Place the scallops on a baking sheet lined with parchment paper.
6. Drizzle with olive oil.
7. Bake for 15-20 minutes or until the scallops are golden brown and cooked through.

Nutrition: Per serving: Approximately 255 calories, 15g fat, 12g carbohydrates, 17g protein.

TRADITIONAL BRUSCHETTA WITH FRESH TOMATOES

Cook Time: 10 minutes
Serving: 4
Ingredients:
- 4 large ripe tomatoes, chopped
- 4 cloves of garlic, minced
- 1/4 cup of fresh basil leaves, chopped
- 4 tablespoons of extra-virgin olive oil
- 4 slices of rustic bread, cut into 1-inch thick slices
- Salt and pepper, to taste
- Balsamic glaze, optional

Preparation:
1. In a medium bowl, mix together the chopped tomatoes, minced garlic, basil leaves, 2 tablespoons of olive oil, salt, and pepper. Set aside.
2. Brush both sides of each bread slice with remaining olive oil.
3. Toast the bread slices on a griddle or in a toaster oven until they are golden brown.
4. Rub each toasted bread slice with a garlic clove.
5. Spoon the tomato mixture onto each bread slice and spread evenly.
6. Serve immediately and drizzle with balsamic glaze, if desired.

Nutrition: (per serving) Calories: 250 Fat: 16g Saturated Fat: 2.5g Cholesterol: 0mg Sodium: 340mg Carbohydrates: 25g Fiber: 3g Sugar: 5g Protein: 6g

CROSTINI WITH PROSCIUTTO AND BURRATA

Cook time: 15 minutes
Serving: 4
Ingredients:
- 4 slices of prosciutto
- 1 burrata cheese
- 8 slices of crusty bread
- 2 tablespoons of olive oil
- Salt and pepper to taste

Preparation:
1. Preheat the oven to 400°F.
2. Place the crusty bread slices on a baking sheet and brush both sides with olive oil.
3. Bake the bread slices in the oven for 8-10 minutes until crispy and golden.
4. While the bread is in the oven, place the prosciutto on a separate baking sheet and bake for 5-7 minutes until crispy.
5. Remove both the bread and prosciutto from the oven and let them cool.
6. Place a slice of burrata cheese on top of each slice of toasted bread.
7. Top each slice with a slice of crispy prosciutto.
8. Sprinkle with salt and pepper to taste.
9. Serve immediately.

Nutrition (per serving): Calories: 400 Fat: 29g Protein: 19g Carbohydrates: 19g Fiber: 2g Sugar: 1g

MOZZARELLE IN CARROZZA VENETIAN FRIED MOZZARELLA SANDWICHES

Cook time: 10 minutes
Serving: 4
Ingredients:
- 8 slices of white bread
- 8 thin slices of mozzarella cheese
- 1/2 cup all-purpose flour
- 2 eggs, beaten
- 1 cup breadcrumbs
- Salt and pepper to taste
- Olive oil for frying
- Arugula leaves for garnish

Preparation:
1. Place a slice of mozzarella cheese between two slices of white bread and press the edges together to make a sandwich. Repeat with the remaining slices of bread and cheese.
2. Place the flour in a shallow dish and the beaten eggs in another shallow dish.
3. Season the breadcrumbs with salt and pepper and place in another shallow dish.
4. Dip each sandwich in the flour, then the eggs, and finally in the breadcrumbs. Make sure each sandwich is well coated with breadcrumbs.
5. Heat a large skillet over medium heat and add enough olive oil to cover the bottom of the pan.
6. Fry the sandwiches until they are golden brown, about 2-3 minutes on each side.
7. Serve hot with a handful of arugula leaves on top.

Nutrition (per serving): Calories: 600 Fat: 37 g Carbohydrates: 44 g Protein: 26 g Sodium: 1210 mg

FRITTATA ALLE CIPOLLE ONION FRITTATA

Cook time: 25 minutes
Serving: 4-6
Ingredients:
- 6 large eggs
- 1 medium onion, diced
- 1/4 cup grated Parmesan cheese
- 1/4 teaspoon salt
- 1/4 teaspoon black pepper
- 2 tablespoons olive oil

Preparation:
1. In a large bowl, beat the eggs together.
2. Add the diced onion, grated Parmesan cheese, salt, and pepper to the eggs. Mix well.
3. In a large non-stick frying pan, heat the olive oil over medium heat.
4. Pour the egg mixture into the pan and cook until the edges start to set, about 5 minutes.
5. Using a spatula, lift the edges of the frittata so that the uncooked eggs can flow to the bottom of the pan.
6. Continue cooking until the top is set, but still slightly runny, about 5 minutes more.
7. Place the pan under the broiler for 1-2 minutes, or until the top is golden brown.
8. Slide the frittata onto a large plate and cut into wedges. Serve hot.

Nutrition (per serving, based on 6 servings): Calories: 205 Fat: 17 g Saturated Fat: 4 g Cholesterol: 222 mg Sodium: 384 mg Carbohydrates: 4 g Fiber: 1 g Sugar: 2 g Protein: 12 g

FRITTATA DI SPAGHETTI NEAPOLITAN SPAGHETTI FRITTATA

Cook time: 20 minutes
Serving: 4-6 portions
Ingredients:
- 1 pound spaghetti, cooked and cooled
- 6 large eggs, beaten
- 1/2 cup milk
- 1/2 cup grated Parmesan cheese
- 1/2 cup diced ham
- 1/2 cup diced onion
- 1/2 cup diced red bell pepper
- 2 cloves of garlic, minced
- Salt and pepper, to taste
- 1/4 cup olive oil

Preparation:
1. In a large bowl, beat together eggs, milk, Parmesan cheese, salt, and pepper.
2. In a large skillet, heat olive oil over medium heat. Add diced ham, onion, red bell pepper, and garlic. Cook for about 3-4 minutes until softened.
3. Stir in cooked spaghetti into the skillet and pour egg mixture over the spaghetti.
4. Use a spatula to gently lift the edges of the frittata and let the uncooked egg run to the bottom of the skillet.
5. Cook the frittata for about 8-10 minutes or until the edges start to firm up.
6. Place the skillet in the oven and broil for 3-5 minutes, or until the top of the frittata is golden and the eggs are fully set.
7. Remove from the oven and let it cool for a few minutes. Serve hot.

Nutrition (per serving): Calories: 400 Fat: 25g Carbohydrates: 25g Protein: 20g Fiber: 2g

SOUPS AND SALADS

PASTA E FAGIOLI ALLA VENETA VENETIAN-STYLE BEANS AND PASTA SOUP

Cook time: 30 minutes
Serving: 4
Ingredients:
- 1 cup dried cannellini beans
- 2 tbsp olive oil
- 1 onion, diced
- 2 cloves garlic, minced
- 2 carrots, diced
- 2 celery stalks, diced
- 1 tsp dried thyme
- 1 tsp dried rosemary
- 1/2 tsp dried basil
- 6 cups vegetable broth
- 1 cup ditalini pasta
- Salt and pepper to taste
- Fresh parsley leaves for garnish

Preparation:
1. Rinse the cannellini beans and soak them in water overnight.
2. In a large saucepan, heat the olive oil over medium heat.
3. Add the onion, garlic, carrots, and celery and sauté until the onion is soft and translucent, about 5 minutes.
4. Add the thyme, rosemary, and basil to the pan and continue to cook for another minute.
5. Drain the beans and add them to the pan along with the vegetable broth.
6. Bring the mixture to a boil and then reduce the heat to low and simmer for 20 minutes.
7. Add the ditalini pasta to the soup and cook until al dente, about 8-10 minutes.
8. Season the soup with salt and pepper to taste.
9. Serve the soup hot, garnished with fresh parsley leaves.

Nutrition: Per serving: 300 calories, 8g fat, 46g carbohydrates, 14g protein.

MINESTRONE SOUP

Cook time: 45 minutes
Serving: 6-8
Ingredients:
- 1 large onion, chopped
- 2 celery stalks, chopped
- 2 carrots, chopped
- 3 cloves of garlic, minced
- 2 tablespoons olive oil
- 1 can (28 ounces) of diced tomatoes
- 4 cups of chicken or vegetable broth
- 1 cup of green beans
- 1 cup of cooked elbow macaroni

- 1 can (15 ounces) of kidney beans
- 1 can (15 ounces) of chickpeas
- 1 teaspoon dried basil
- 1 teaspoon dried oregano
- Salt and pepper to taste

Preparation:
1. In a large pot, heat the olive oil over medium heat.
2. Add the onions, celery, carrots, and garlic. Cook until the vegetables are soft, about 5 minutes.
3. Add the canned tomatoes, broth, green beans, macaroni, kidney beans, chickpeas, basil, oregano, salt, and pepper.
4. Stir to combine and bring to a boil.
5. Reduce heat to a simmer and cook for 30 minutes, or until all the vegetables are tender.
6. Serve hot with a piece of crusty bread.

Nutrition (per serving based on 8 servings): Calories: 215 Fat: 7g Saturated Fat: 1g Cholesterol: 0mg Sodium: 548mg Carbohydrates: 31g Fiber: 7g Sugar: 7g Protein: 9g

PASTA E CECI CHICKPEAS AND PASTA SOUP

Cook time: 30 minutes
Serving: 4
Ingredients:
- 1 cup dried chickpeas, soaked overnight
- 4 cups chicken or vegetable broth
- 1 onion, chopped
- 2 cloves garlic, minced
- 1 cup canned tomatoes, chopped
- 1/2 tsp dried basil
- 1/2 tsp dried thyme
- Salt and pepper to taste
- 1 cup small pasta, such as ditalini
- Grated Parmesan cheese, for serving (optional)

Preparation:
1. In a large saucepan, combine the chickpeas, broth, onion, garlic, tomatoes, basil, thyme, salt, and pepper. Bring to a boil over high heat.
2. Reduce heat to low, cover, and simmer until the chickpeas are tender, about 20 minutes.
3. Add the pasta and cook until al dente, about 8 minutes.
4. Serve hot, topped with Parmesan cheese if desired.

Nutrition: Per serving (without cheese): Calories: 239 Fat: 2.5 g Saturated Fat: 0.5 g Cholesterol: 0 mg Sodium: 422 mg Carbohydrates: 42 g Fiber: 9 g Sugar: 5 g Protein: 12 g

RIBOLLITA TUSCAN KALE AND BREAD SOUP

Cook time: 1 hour
Serving: 6-8
Ingredients:
- 1 large onion, chopped
- 3 carrots, diced

- 3 stalks celery, diced
- 4 cloves garlic, minced
- 3 tablespoons olive oil
- 2 cans (14.5 ounces each) diced tomatoes
- 1 bunch kale, chopped
- 6 cups chicken or vegetable broth
- 2 cups cooked cannellini beans
- Salt and pepper to taste
- 1 loaf of crusty bread, torn into bite-sized pieces
- Parmesan cheese, grated for garnish

Preparation:
1. In a large pot, heat the olive oil over medium heat. Add the onion, carrots, celery, and garlic and cook until the vegetables are soft, about 10 minutes.
2. Add the diced tomatoes and kale to the pot and cook for another 5 minutes.
3. Pour in the broth and bring to a boil. Add the cooked cannellini beans and reduce heat to a simmer. Let cook for 30 minutes.
4. Season with salt and pepper to taste.
5. In a separate pan, toast the bread until crisp and golden.
6. To serve, ladle the soup into bowls and top with the toasted bread and grated Parmesan cheese.

Nutrition (per serving): Approximately 200 calories 9 grams of fat 22 grams of carbohydrates 11 grams of protein.

PASSATELLI IN BRODO HOMEMADE PASSATELLI PASTA IN BROTH FROM EMILIA

Cook Time: 25 minutes
Servings: 4
Ingredients:
- 1 lb. of all-purpose flour
- 2 large eggs
- 1 tsp. of salt
- 1 tsp. of grated Parmesan cheese
- 3 cups of chicken or beef broth
- 2 tbsp. of olive oil
- Salt and pepper to taste

Preparation:
1. In a large bowl, mix the flour, eggs, salt, and grated Parmesan cheese until a dough forms. If the dough is too sticky, add a little bit more flour.
2. Roll the dough into a sausage shape, then cut it into small pieces about 1 inch in length.
3. Roll each piece of dough into a long, thin rope, then cut into small pieces about 1 inch in length.
4. Using a fork, gently press down on each piece of dough to create a ridged surface.
5. In a large saucepan, heat the broth and olive oil over medium heat.
6. Once the broth starts to simmer, drop the passatelli into the pan and stir gently. Cook for about 5-7 minutes, or until the pasta floats to the surface.
7. Season with salt and pepper to taste, then serve hot in bowls.

Nutrition (per serving): Calories: 350 kcal Protein: 14 g Fat: 8 g Carbohydrates: 54 g Sugar: 1 g Fiber: 2 g Sodium: 720 mg

ZUPPA D'ORZO BARLEY SOUP FROM ALTO ADIGE

Cook time: 30 minutes
Serving: 4
Ingredients:
- 2 tablespoons olive oil
- 1 onion, chopped
- 2 cloves garlic, minced
- 1 carrot, diced
- 1 celery stalk, diced
- 1 cup barley
- 6 cups chicken or vegetable broth
- 1 cup diced tomato
- Salt and pepper to taste
- Fresh parsley for garnish (optional)

Preparation:
1. Heat the olive oil in a large pot over medium heat.
2. Add the onion and garlic and cook until the onion is translucent, about 5 minutes.
3. Add the carrot and celery and cook for another 5 minutes.
4. Add the barley and cook for 2 minutes, stirring constantly.
5. Add the broth and bring to a boil.
6. Reduce heat to low and simmer for 20 minutes, or until the barley is tender.
7. Add the diced tomato and cook for another 5 minutes.
8. Season with salt and pepper to taste.
9. Serve hot, garnished with fresh parsley if desired.

Nutrition (per serving): Calories: 242 Fat: 11g Protein: 10g Carbohydrates: 29g Fiber: 5g Sugar: 3g

CAPRESE SALAD

Cook time: 10 minutes
Serving: 4
Ingredients:
- 4 ripe tomatoes
- 8 ounces fresh mozzarella cheese
- 2 tablespoons extra virgin olive oil
- 2 tablespoons balsamic vinegar
- Salt and pepper to taste
- Fresh basil leaves for garnish

Preparation:
1. Slice the tomatoes and mozzarella cheese into thin rounds.
2. Arrange the tomato and cheese slices alternately on a serving platter.
3. In a small bowl, whisk together the olive oil, balsamic vinegar, salt and pepper.
4. Drizzle the dressing over the top of the salad.
5. Garnish with fresh basil leaves.
6. Serve immediately.

Nutrition (per serving): Calories: 230 Fat: 18g Protein: 12g Carbs: 8g Sodium: 530mg

RADICCHIO, ARUGULA, AND SHAVED FENNEL SALAD WITH ANCHOVY

Cook time: 10 minutes

Serving: 4

Ingredients:
- 4 cups of radicchio leaves, chopped
- 2 cups of arugula leaves
- 1 medium fennel bulb, shaved
- 6 anchovy fillets, minced
- 2 tablespoons of lemon juice
- 2 tablespoons of olive oil
- Salt and pepper, to taste

Preparation:
1. Rinse and chop the radicchio leaves, and place them in a large mixing bowl.
2. Add the arugula leaves to the bowl and set aside.
3. Shave the fennel bulb using a mandoline or a sharp knife.
4. In a small mixing bowl, whisk together the lemon juice, olive oil, anchovy fillets, salt, and pepper.
5. Pour the dressing over the radicchio and arugula, and toss to combine.
6. Add the shaved fennel to the salad, and toss again to mix.
7. Serve immediately, garnished with extra anchovy fillets if desired.

Nutrition (per serving): Calories: 140 Fat: 14g Protein: 4g Carbohydrates: 7g Fiber: 3g Sugar: 2g Sodium: 476mg

VINAIGRETTE

Cook time: 5 minutes

Serving: 4-6

Ingredients:
- 1/2 cup olive oil
- 1/4 cup red wine vinegar
- 1 teaspoon Dijon mustard
- 1 garlic clove, minced
- Salt and pepper to taste
- Optional: 1 tablespoon honey or 1 teaspoon sugar

Preparation:
1. In a small bowl, whisk together the red wine vinegar, Dijon mustard, minced garlic, salt, and pepper.
2. Gradually add the olive oil while continuously whisking until the mixture emulsifies.
3. If using honey or sugar, whisk it into the mixture until fully incorporated.
4. Taste and adjust seasonings as needed.
5. Serve immediately or store in a sealed container in the refrigerator for up to a week.

Nutrition (per serving, based on 6 servings): Calories: 170 Fat: 18g Saturated Fat: 2.5g Cholesterol: 0mg Sodium: 30mg Carbohydrates: 1g Protein: 0g

CAPONATA DI TONNO NEAPOLITAN TUNA, TOMATO, AND BREAD SALAD

Cook time: 25 minutes

Serving: 4
Ingredients:
- 2 cans of Neapolitan Tuna, drained
- 2 medium sized tomatoes, diced
- 2 slices of day-old bread, cut into small cubes
- 1 medium sized eggplant, diced
- 1 red bell pepper, diced
- 1 yellow onion, diced
- 1/4 cup of green olives, pitted and chopped
- 2 tablespoons of capers, drained
- 2 cloves of garlic, minced
- 2 tablespoons of red wine vinegar
- 2 tablespoons of extra virgin olive oil
- Salt and pepper to taste
- Fresh basil leaves for garnish (optional)

Preparation:
1. In a large pan, heat the olive oil over medium heat.
2. Add the diced eggplant and cook until it is golden brown, about 8 minutes.
3. Add the diced onion and red bell pepper to the pan and cook until the onion is translucent, about 5 minutes.
4. Add the minced garlic and cook for another minute.
5. Add the canned tuna to the pan and cook for about 3 minutes, breaking it apart with a wooden spoon.
6. Add the diced tomatoes, chopped olives, and capers to the pan. Stir to combine.
7. Pour in the red wine vinegar and stir.
8. Add the bread cubes to the pan and stir until well combined.
9. Season with salt and pepper to taste.
10. Transfer the caponata to a serving dish and let it cool to room temperature.
11. Serve the caponata with fresh basil leaves for garnish (optional).

Nutrition: (per serving) Calories: 250 Fat: 15 g Saturated Fat: 2 g Cholesterol: 30 mg Sodium: 580 mg Carbohydrates: 17 g Fiber: 4 gSugar: 8 g Protein: 16 g

INSALATA DI FINOCCHI E ARANCE SICILIAN FENNEL AND ORANGE SALAD

Cook time: 10 minutes
Serving: 4-6 people
Ingredients:
- 2 medium sized fennel bulbs, thinly sliced
- 2 medium sized oranges, peeled and segmented
- 1/4 cup chopped fresh parsley
- 2 tablespoons olive oil
- 1 tablespoon white wine vinegar
- Salt and pepper to taste
- 1/4 cup toasted almonds (optional)

Preparation:
1. Slice the fennel bulbs thinly and add them to a large salad bowl.
2. Peel and segment the oranges, removing all the pith, and add them to the bowl with the fennel.

3. Add chopped parsley, olive oil, white wine vinegar, salt and pepper to the bowl.
4. Toss everything together to combine.
5. If desired, sprinkle toasted almonds on top before serving.

Nutrition: Serving size: 1/6 of recipe Calories: 99 Fat: 7g Carbohydrates: 10g Protein: 2g Sodium: 73mg

PANZANELLA TUSCAN BREAD AND TOMATO SALAD

Cook Time: 20 minutes
Serving: 4 people
Ingredients:
- 4 cups of bread, cut into 1 inch cubes
- 2 large ripe tomatoes, diced
- 1 red onion, thinly sliced
- 1 cucumber, peeled and diced
- 1 red bell pepper, diced
- 1 yellow bell pepper, diced
- 1/4 cup of red wine vinegar
- 1/4 cup of extra virgin olive oil
- 1/4 cup of chopped basil leaves
- Salt and pepper to taste

Preparation:
1. Preheat oven to 375°F.
2. Place the bread cubes on a baking sheet and toast in the oven for 10-12 minutes, or until they are golden brown and crispy.
3. In a large bowl, mix together the diced tomatoes, red onion, cucumber, red and yellow bell peppers.
4. In a separate bowl, mix together the red wine vinegar, extra virgin olive oil, basil leaves, salt, and pepper to make the dressing.
5. Add the toasted bread cubes to the vegetable mixture and mix well.
6. Pour the dressing over the bread and vegetable mixture and toss to coat everything evenly.
7. Let the salad sit for 10 minutes to allow the bread to soak up the dressing.
8. Serve the panzanella salad chilled or at room temperature.

Nutrition (per serving): Calories: 261 Fat: 15 g Sodium: 466 mg Carbohydrates: 28 g Protein: 6 g

FARRO SALAD

Cook time: 20 minutes
Serving: 4-6
Ingredients:
- 1 cup farro
- 1 red bell pepper, diced
- 1 yellow bell pepper, diced
- 1/2 cup cherry tomatoes, halved
- 1/2 cup diced cucumber
- 1/2 cup crumbled feta cheese
- 1/4 cup chopped fresh basil
- 1/4 cup olive oil

- 2 tablespoons lemon juice
- salt and pepper to taste

Preparation:
1. Cook farro according to package instructions until tender, about 20 minutes. Drain and let cool.
2. In a large bowl, mix together the farro, red and yellow bell peppers, cherry tomatoes, cucumber, feta cheese, and basil.
3. In a separate bowl, whisk together the olive oil and lemon juice. Season with salt and pepper to taste.
4. Pour the dressing over the farro mixture and toss to combine. Serve at room temperature.

Nutrition (per serving, based on 6 servings): Calories: 350 Fat: 22g Carbohydrates: 34g Protein: 10g Sodium: 550mg Fiber: 4g

RISOTTO AND POLENTA

RISOTTO ALLA MILANESE RISOTTO WITH SAFFRON

Cook time: 30 minutes
Servings: 4
Ingredients:
- 1 1/2 cups Arborio rice
- 1 large onion, chopped
- 2 cloves garlic, minced
- 4 cups chicken or vegetable broth
- 1/2 cup white wine
- 1/2 teaspoon saffron threads
- 1/2 cup grated Parmesan cheese
- 2 tablespoons unsalted butter
- Salt and pepper, to taste
- Optional: chopped parsley for garnish

Preparation:
1. In a large saucepan, heat the broth over low heat.
2. In another saucepan, heat 2 tablespoons of butter over medium heat. Add the onions and garlic and cook until the onions are translucent, about 5 minutes.
3. Add the rice to the saucepan with the onions and cook for 2 minutes, stirring constantly, until the rice is slightly toasted.
4. Pour in the wine and cook until the wine has been absorbed by the rice.
5. Stir in the saffron threads.
6. Gradually add the warm broth to the rice, about 1/2 cup at a time, stirring constantly until each addition has been absorbed before adding the next. Continue until the broth has been used up and the rice is creamy and tender, about 20 minutes.
7. Stir in the grated Parmesan cheese and remaining 2 tablespoons of butter.
8. Season with salt and pepper, to taste.
9. Serve immediately, garnished with chopped parsley if desired.

Nutrition: (per serving) Calories: 365 Fat: 15g Saturated Fat: 8g Cholesterol: 35mg Sodium: 992mg Carbohydrates: 46g Fiber: 1g Sugar: 2g Protein: 9g.

RISOTTO WITH PORCINI MUSHROOMS

Cook time: 30 minutes
Serving: 4-6 people
Ingredients:
- 1 oz. dried porcini mushrooms
- 4 cups chicken or vegetable broth
- 1 large onion, diced
- 2 cloves of garlic, minced
- 1 cup arborio rice
- 1/2 cup white wine
- 1/2 cup grated Parmesan cheese

- 2 tablespoons butter
- Salt and pepper to taste

Preparation:
1. Soak the dried porcini mushrooms in 2 cups of warm water for 30 minutes. Reserve the soaking liquid and strain out any grit.
2. In a saucepan, heat the broth until it's warm and keep it on low heat.
3. In a large saucepan, heat the butter over medium heat. Add the onion and garlic and cook until softened, about 5 minutes.
4. Add the rice and cook for 2-3 minutes, stirring frequently.
5. Pour in the wine and stir until it's absorbed.
6. Add the soaked porcini mushrooms and the strained soaking liquid to the saucepan, a ladleful at a time, stirring constantly until the liquid is absorbed. Repeat until all the broth has been added and the rice is creamy and tender, about 20-25 minutes.
7. Stir in the Parmesan cheese and season with salt and pepper to taste. Serve immediately.

Nutrition: (per serving) Calories: 305 Fat: 11 g Carbohydrates: 38 g Protein: 12 g Fiber: 2 g.

RISOTTO WITH RADICCHIO AND SAUSAGE

Cook Time: 30 minutes
Serving: 4-6 people
Ingredients:
- 1 lb sweet Italian sausage, removed from casings
- 1 medium onion, chopped
- 2 garlic cloves, minced
- 1 cup arborio rice
- 1/2 cup white wine
- 4 cups chicken or vegetable broth
- 1 head of radicchio, sliced
- 1/2 cup grated Parmesan cheese
- 2 tablespoons butter
- Salt and pepper, to taste

Preparation:
1. In a large saucepan, cook the sausage over medium heat, breaking it up into small pieces as it browns. Once cooked, remove from the pan and set aside.
2. In the same pan, add the chopped onion and garlic and cook until the onion is translucent.
3. Add the arborio rice and cook, stirring frequently, for 2-3 minutes until the rice is opaque.
4. Pour in the white wine and cook, stirring, until it has been absorbed.
5. Begin adding the chicken or vegetable broth, 1 cup at a time, stirring constantly until each cup has been absorbed before adding the next. Continue until all the broth has been added and the rice is creamy.
6. Stir in the cooked sausage and sliced radicchio. Cook until the radicchio has wilted, about 2-3 minutes.
7. Stir in the Parmesan cheese and butter, and season with salt and pepper to taste.
8. Serve hot and garnish with additional Parmesan cheese, if desired.

Nutrition (per serving, based on 6 servings): Calories: 464 Fat: 27g Carbohydrates: 33g Protein: 22g Sodium: 1076mg

RISOTTO ALLO SCOGLIO SEAFOOD RISOTTO

Cook time: 30 minutes
Serving: 4 portions
Ingredients:
- 1 onion, finely chopped
- 2 garlic cloves, minced
- 1 cup arborio rice
- 4 cups chicken broth
- 1 cup white wine
- 1 pound mixed seafood (shrimp, scallops, mussels, calamari)
- 1/2 cup grated parmesan cheese
- 2 tbsp olive oil
- Salt and pepper to taste
- Fresh parsley for garnish

Preparation:
1. In a large pan, heat the olive oil over medium heat. Add the onion and garlic and cook until soft and translucent, about 5 minutes.
2. Stir in the arborio rice, making sure it is well coated with the oil. Cook for 2 minutes, stirring constantly.
3. Add the white wine and cook until the liquid is absorbed, about 3 minutes.
4. Begin adding the chicken broth, a cup at a time, stirring continuously until the liquid is absorbed before adding more. Repeat this process until all the broth has been used and the rice is cooked, about 20 minutes.
5. Add the mixed seafood and cook until the shrimp and scallops are opaque and the mussels have opened, about 5 minutes.
6. Stir in the parmesan cheese and season with salt and pepper to taste.
7. Serve hot, garnished with fresh parsley.

Nutrition: (per serving) Calories: 470 Fat: 19g Saturated Fat: 7g Cholesterol: 135mg Sodium: 1300mg Carbohydrates: 46g Fiber: 2g Sugar: 3g Protein: 29g

RISOTTO AL SALTO CRISPY RICE CAKE

Cook time: 25-30 minutes
Serving: 4
Ingredients:
- 1 1/2 cups arborio rice
- 4 cups chicken or vegetable broth
- 1/2 onion, diced
- 2 garlic cloves, minced
- 1/2 cup white wine
- 1/2 cup grated parmesan cheese
- 2 tbsp butter
- 2 tbsp olive oil
- Salt and pepper to taste

Preparation:
1. In a large saucepan, heat 2 tbsp of olive oil and 2 tbsp of butter over medium heat.

2. Add the diced onion and minced garlic and cook until softened, about 5 minutes.
3. Add the arborio rice to the saucepan and stir for 2-3 minutes until the rice is coated with the oil and butter mixture.
4. Pour in the white wine and cook until the wine has been absorbed by the rice.
5. Slowly add the chicken or vegetable broth, one ladleful at a time, stirring continuously until the liquid has been absorbed before adding the next ladleful.
6. Continue to stir and add broth until the rice is cooked to your liking, approximately 20 minutes.
7. Stir in the grated parmesan cheese and season with salt and pepper to taste.
8. Remove from heat and let the risotto cool for 10 minutes.
9. In a large, non-stick pan, heat a thin layer of oil over medium heat.
10. Scoop 1/4 cup portions of the cooled risotto into the pan, flattening each portion into a pancake shape.
11. Cook the rice cakes for 2-3 minutes on each side until crispy and golden brown.
12. Serve hot with your favorite toppings or sauce.

Nutrition: Serving size: 1 crispy rice cake Calories: 264 Fat: 14 g Carbohydrates: 26 g Protein: 7 g

RISOTTO WITH SHRIMP AND ASPARAGUS

Cook time: 30 minutes
Serving: 4
Ingredients:
- 1 cup arborio rice
- 1 onion, chopped
- 3 garlic cloves, minced
- 1 cup white wine
- 4 cups chicken or vegetable broth
- 1 lb. large shrimp, peeled and deveined
- 1 lb. asparagus, trimmed and cut into 1 inch pieces
- 1/2 cup grated Parmesan cheese
- 2 tbsp. olive oil
- Salt and pepper to taste
- Fresh parsley for garnish

Preparation:
1. Heat the olive oil in a large saucepan over medium heat.
2. Add the onion and cook until translucent, about 5 minutes.
3. Add the garlic and cook for another minute.
4. Stir in the arborio rice and cook for 2 minutes, until slightly toasted.
5. Pour in the white wine and cook, stirring frequently, until the liquid has been absorbed.
6. Gradually add the chicken or vegetable broth, one cup at a time, stirring constantly until each cup has been absorbed before adding the next.
7. After adding the last cup of broth, stir in the shrimp and asparagus.
8. Cook until the shrimp is pink and the asparagus is tender, about 5-7 minutes.
9. Stir in the Parmesan cheese and season with salt and pepper to taste.
10. Serve hot, garnished with fresh parsley.

Nutrition:

Each serving contains approximately 450 calories, with 17g of fat, 43g of carbohydrates, and 27g of protein.

RISI E BISI VENETO-STYLE RICE AND PEAS

Cook time: 30 minutes
Serving: 4-6
Ingredients:
- 1 cup arborio rice
- 2 cups vegetable broth
- 1 cup fresh or frozen green peas
- 1 small onion, diced
- 2 cloves garlic, minced
- 1/4 cup pancetta or bacon, diced
- 2 tablespoons olive oil
- 1/2 teaspoon salt
- 1/4 teaspoon black pepper
- 1/4 cup grated Parmesan cheese
- 2 tablespoons butter
- 1/4 cup chopped fresh parsley

Preparation:
1. In a large saucepan, heat the olive oil over medium heat. Add the onion and garlic and cook until softened, about 5 minutes.
2. Add the pancetta or bacon and cook for an additional 5 minutes, or until crisp.
3. Add the rice and stir well to coat it with the oil. Cook for 2 minutes until the rice is lightly toasted.
4. Add the vegetable broth and bring to a boil. Reduce heat and cover the saucepan. Cook for 15 minutes, or until the liquid is absorbed and the rice is tender.
5. Add the green peas and cook for another 5 minutes.
6. Stir in the Parmesan cheese and butter until melted.
7. Stir in the parsley and serve hot.

Nutrition: Per serving (based on 6 servings) Calories: 327 Fat: 17g Carbohydrates: 35g Protein: 10g Fiber: 3g Sodium: 726mg

BASIC POLENTA

Cook time: 45 minutes
Serving: 4-6
Ingredients:
- 4 cups water
- 1 teaspoon salt
- 1 cup coarse cornmeal
- 1/4 cup grated Parmesan cheese
- 2 tablespoons butter

Preparation:
1. Bring the water and salt to a boil in a medium saucepan over high heat.
2. Gradually pour in the cornmeal, whisking constantly to prevent lumps.
3. Reduce the heat to low and continue to whisk the mixture for about 30-35 minutes, until it starts to pull away from the sides of the pan.

4. Stir in the Parmesan cheese and butter until melted and well combined.
5. Serve immediately with your favorite sauce or toppings.

Nutrition (per serving, based on 6 servings): Calories: 179 Total Fat: 9.6 g Saturated Fat: 5.4 g Cholesterol: 24 mg Sodium: 686 mg Total Carbohydrates: 17.8 g Dietary Fiber: 2 g Sugar: 0.5 g Protein: 5.5 g

GRILLED POLENTA

Cook time: 20 minutes
Serving: 4
Ingredients:
- 4 cups of water
- 1 cup of cornmeal
- 2 tbsp of olive oil
- 1 tsp of salt
- 1 tsp of black pepper
- 2 tbsp of grated Parmesan cheese (optional)

Preparation:
1. In a large saucepan, bring the water to a boil over medium-high heat.
2. Slowly pour in the cornmeal while whisking continuously to prevent lumps.
3. Reduce heat to medium-low and cook for 10 to 15 minutes, stirring frequently, until the mixture thickens.
4. Stir in the olive oil, salt, black pepper, and grated Parmesan cheese (if using).
5. Pour the mixture into a greased 9x13 inch baking dish. Spread evenly and let it cool.
6. Once cooled, cut the polenta into squares or rectangles and place on a hot grill.
7. Cook for 3 to 5 minutes on each side or until slightly crispy.
8. Serve hot with your desired toppings such as marinara sauce, sautéed vegetables, or grilled meats.

Nutrition (per serving): Calories: 220 Fat: 8g Saturated Fat: 2g Cholesterol: 5mg Sodium: 420mg Carbohydrates: 33g Fiber: 2g Protein: 6g

BAKED POLENTA WITH CHEESE, MUSHROOMS, AND SAUSAGE

Cook time: 50 minutes
Serving: 4-6
Ingredients:
- 1 cup polenta
- 4 cups chicken or vegetable broth
- 1 cup grated Parmesan cheese
- 1/2 cup heavy cream
- 1 teaspoon salt
- 1/4 teaspoon black pepper
- 1 teaspoon olive oil
- 1/2 pound sausage, sliced
- 8 ounces mushrooms, sliced
- 1/4 cup chopped fresh parsley
- 1/4 cup chopped fresh basil

Preparation:

1. Preheat the oven to 375°F (190°C). Grease a 9x13 inch baking dish.
2. In a medium saucepan, bring the broth to a boil. Gradually whisk in the polenta. Cook, stirring constantly, for 5 minutes or until the polenta is thick and smooth.
3. Remove the pan from heat and stir in the Parmesan cheese, heavy cream, salt, and pepper.
4. Pour the mixture into the prepared baking dish and smooth out the top with a spatula. Bake for 25 minutes or until set.
5. In a large skillet, heat the olive oil over medium heat. Add the sausage and cook for 8-10 minutes, stirring occasionally, until browned. Remove from heat.
6. In the same skillet, add the sliced mushrooms and cook for 5 minutes or until tender.
7. Cut the baked polenta into squares and top with the cooked sausage and mushrooms. Sprinkle with the chopped parsley and basil. Serve immediately.

Nutrition: (per serving, based on 6 servings) Calorie: 494 Fat: 38.6g Saturated Fat: 17.8g Cholesterol: 111mg Sodium: 1094mg Carbohydrates: 16.3g Fiber: 2.3g Sugar: 1.2g Protein: 24.9g.

SAUCES AND PASTA

BASIC TOMATO SAUCE

Cook time: 30 minutes
Serving: 4 servings
Ingredients:
- 1 tablespoon olive oil
- 1 onion, chopped
- 2 cloves garlic, minced
- 1 can (28 ounces) whole tomatoes, chopped
- 1 teaspoon sugar
- Salt and pepper, to taste
- Fresh basil leaves, chopped (optional)

Preparation:
1. Heat the olive oil in a medium saucepan over medium heat.
2. Add the chopped onion and cook until soft, about 5 minutes.
3. Add the minced garlic and cook for another minute.
4. Add the chopped tomatoes and their juice, sugar, salt, and pepper to the saucepan.
5. Stir to combine and bring to a boil.
6. Reduce heat to low and let the sauce simmer for 20 minutes, stirring occasionally.
7. Remove from heat and let cool slightly.
8. Blend the sauce using an immersion blender or transfer to a blender and blend until smooth.
9. Stir in chopped basil leaves if desired.

Nutrition (per serving): Calories: 79 Fat: 4g Saturated Fat: 0.5g Cholesterol: 0mg Sodium: 226mg Carbohydrates: 12g Fiber: 3g Sugar: 7g Protein: 2g

RAVI ALLA BOLOGNESE MEAT SAUCE

Cook time: 1 hour and 30 minutes
Serving: 6-8 portions
Ingredients:
- 1 pound ground beef
- 1 onion, diced
- 2 garlic cloves, minced
- 1 can (14.5 ounces) of diced tomatoes
- 1 cup beef broth
- 1 teaspoon dried basil
- 1 teaspoon dried oregano
- 1 teaspoon salt
- 1/2 teaspoon black pepper
- 1/2 teaspoon red pepper flakes (optional)
- 1/4 cup red wine
- 1 tablespoon tomato paste
- 1/4 cup heavy cream
- 1/4 cup grated parmesan cheese
- 1/2 pound spaghetti or other pasta of choice

Preparation:
1. In a large pot, heat a small amount of oil over medium heat. Add the diced onions and cook until soft, about 5 minutes.
2. Add the minced garlic and cook for another minute.
3. Add the ground beef to the pot and cook until browned, breaking up any large clumps with a wooden spoon.
4. Pour in the diced tomatoes, beef broth, dried basil, dried oregano, salt, pepper, and red pepper flakes. Stir well to combine.
5. Add the red wine, tomato paste, and heavy cream to the pot and stir to combine.
6. Reduce heat to low and let the sauce simmer for 1 hour, stirring occasionally.
7. In a separate pot, cook the spaghetti or pasta according to package instructions.
8. Drain the pasta and add it to the sauce. Toss to combine.
9. Serve with a sprinkle of grated parmesan cheese on top.

Nutrition: (per serving) Calories: 360 Total Fat: 20g Saturated Fat: 9g Cholesterol: 74mg Sodium: 589mg Total Carbohydrates: 25g Dietary Fiber: 3g Sugars: 5g Protein: 20g

PESTO ALLA GENOVESE PESTO SAUCE

Cook time: 15 minutes
Serving: 4
Ingredients:
- 2 cups basil leaves
- 1/2 cup extra-virgin olive oil
- 1/2 cup grated Parmesan cheese
- 1/3 cup pine nuts
- 4 cloves of garlic
- Salt to taste

Preparation:
1. Wash the basil leaves and dry them thoroughly.
2. In a food processor, combine the basil leaves, garlic, pine nuts, and Parmesan cheese.
3. Gradually add the olive oil while blending the ingredients until a smooth paste is formed.
4. Season with salt to taste.
5. Serve with pasta, bread, or as a marinade for meat and vegetables.

Nutrition (per serving): Calories: 380 Fat: 41 g Carbohydrates: 4 g Protein: 7 g Sodium: 300 mg

BESCIAMELLA SAUCE WHITE SAUCE

Cook time: 20 minutes
Serving: 4
Ingredients:
- 2 tablespoons unsalted butter
- 2 tablespoons all-purpose flour
- 2 cups whole milk
- 1/2 teaspoon salt
- 1/4 teaspoon white pepper
- 1/8 teaspoon nutmeg

Preparation:

1. In a medium saucepan, melt the butter over medium heat.
2. Add the flour and whisk together until smooth, about 1 minute.
3. Slowly pour in the milk, whisking constantly to avoid lumps.
4. Increase the heat to medium-high and continue to whisk until the mixture comes to a boil and thickens, about 8 to 10 minutes.
5. Remove from heat and stir in the salt, pepper, and nutmeg.
6. Use as desired.

Nutrition (per serving, based on 4 servings): Calories: 140, Total Fat: 13 g, Saturated Fat: 8 g, Cholesterol: 40 mg, Sodium: 330 mg, Carbohydrates: 6 g, Dietary Fiber: 0 g, Sugar: 4 g, Protein: 4 g.

HOMEMADE EGG TAGLIATELLE PASTA

Cook time: 40 minutes
Serving: 4
Ingredients:
- 2 cups of all-purpose flour
- 3 large eggs
- 1/2 teaspoon of salt
- 1 tablespoon of olive oil

Preparation:
1. In a large mixing bowl, combine 2 cups of all-purpose flour and 1/2 teaspoon of salt.
2. Crack 3 large eggs into the center of the bowl.
3. Add 1 tablespoon of olive oil.
4. Mix the ingredients until it forms into a dough.
5. Knead the dough for about 10 minutes until it becomes smooth and elastic.
6. Cover the dough with plastic wrap and let it rest for about 30 minutes.
7. Roll the dough out on a floured surface into thin sheets.
8. Cut the sheets into thin strips.
9. Bring a large pot of salted water to a boil.
10. Cook the egg tagliatelle pasta for 2-3 minutes or until al dente.
11. Serve with your favorite sauce and enjoy!

Nutrition (per serving): Calories: 309 Fat: 10 g Carbohydrates: 43 g Protein: 11 g Sodium: 421 mg.

HOMEMADE SPINACH RICOTTA RAVIOLI

Cook time: 45 minutes
Serving: 4-6
Ingredients:
- 1 lb. fresh spinach
- 15 oz. ricotta cheese
- 1 egg
- 1 tsp. salt
- 1 tsp. black pepper
- 1 tsp. grated nutmeg
- 1 package fresh pasta sheets
- Flour for dusting

Preparation:

1. Rinse the fresh spinach and chop into small pieces. Cook in boiling water for 2 minutes until wilted. Drain and let cool.
2. In a large mixing bowl, combine the cooked spinach, ricotta cheese, egg, salt, black pepper, and nutmeg. Mix well.
3. Dust a flat surface with flour and lay out the pasta sheets.
4. Using a spoon, place spoonfuls of the spinach and ricotta mixture onto half of the pasta sheet. Leave about 1 inch of space between each spoonful.
5. Fold the other half of the pasta sheet over the filling and press down around each spoonful to seal. Cut into individual ravioli with a knife or ravioli cutter.
6. Repeat this process with the remaining pasta sheets and filling.
7. Bring a large pot of salted water to a boil. Add the ravioli and cook for 4-5 minutes until they float to the surface.
8. Serve with your favorite sauce and grated Parmesan cheese.

Nutrition (per serving, based on 6 servings): Calories: 252 Fat: 11 g Saturated Fat: 6 g Cholesterol: 61 mg Sodium: 519 mg Carbohydrates: 26 g Fiber: 2 g Sugar: 2 g Protein: 13 g

SPAGHETTI ALLA CARBONARA

Cook time: 20 minutes
Serving: 4
Ingredients:
- 1 pound spaghetti
- 6 large eggs
- 1 cup grated Parmesan cheese
- 1 cup pancetta or bacon, diced
- 2 cloves of garlic, minced
- Salt and pepper to taste

Preparation:
1. Cook the spaghetti in a large pot of salted water until al dente, about 8-10 minutes. Drain and set aside.
2. In a large pan, cook the pancetta or bacon over medium heat until crispy, about 8-10 minutes. Remove with a slotted spoon and set aside.
3. In the same pan, add minced garlic and cook for 1-2 minutes until fragrant.
4. In a separate bowl, whisk together the eggs, Parmesan cheese, salt, and pepper.
5. Add the cooked spaghetti to the pan with the garlic and pancetta, and mix well.
6. Remove from heat and add the egg mixture to the pan, tossing quickly to coat the spaghetti evenly.
7. Serve hot and garnish with additional grated Parmesan cheese, if desired.

Nutrition: Per serving (based on 4 servings): Calories: 485 Total Fat: 24g Saturated Fat: 10g Cholesterol: 365mg Sodium: 1,005mg Total Carbohydrates: 40g Dietary Fiber: 2g Sugars: 2g Protein: 25g

PASTA ALL'AMATRICIANA

Cook time: 25 minutes
Serving: 4
Ingredients:
- 1 pound spaghetti

- 4 ounces pancetta, diced
- 1 onion, diced
- 2 garlic cloves, minced
- 2 cans of diced tomatoes
- 1/2 teaspoon red pepper flakes
- Salt and pepper, to taste
- 1/2 cup grated pecorino romano cheese

Preparation:
1. Cook spaghetti according to package instructions. Drain and set aside.
2. In a large pan, heat pancetta over medium heat until crispy.
3. Add onion and garlic to the pan and cook until softened, about 5 minutes.
4. Add the diced tomatoes, red pepper flakes, salt, and pepper to the pan.
5. Cook for about 10 minutes, or until the sauce has thickened.
6. Toss the spaghetti with the sauce.
7. Serve with grated pecorino romano cheese on top.

Nutrition (per serving): Calories: 630 Fat: 20g Carbohydrates: 80g Protein: 26g Sodium: 1740mg Fiber: 4g

CACIO E PEPE CHEESE AND PEPPER PASTA

Cook time: 10 minutes
Serving: 2 people
Ingredients:
- 8 ounces spaghetti
- 1 cup grated Pecorino Romano cheese
- 1 teaspoon freshly ground black pepper
- 1/2 cup reserved pasta water
- Salt, to taste
- Olive oil, to taste

Preparation:
1. Cook the spaghetti in a large pot of salted boiling water according to the package instructions. Reserve 1/2 cup of the pasta water.
2. In a pan, heat 1-2 tablespoons of olive oil over medium heat.
3. Add the ground black pepper and cook for 30 seconds, stirring constantly.
4. Drain the spaghetti and add it to the pan with the black pepper.
5. Add the reserved pasta water and stir to combine.
6. Gradually add the grated Pecorino Romano cheese, stirring continuously until the cheese has melted and the sauce has thickened.
7. Season with salt, to taste.
8. Serve the pasta hot, with extra cheese and pepper on top, if desired.

Nutrition (per serving): Calories: 526 Fat: 22g Sodium: 1080mg Carbohydrates: 61g Fiber: 3g Sugar: 3g Protein: 22g

PENNE ALLA VODKA PENNE PASTA WITH VODKA SAUCE

Cook Time: 20-25 minutes
Serving: 4
Ingredients:

- 1 pound penne pasta
- 1 tablespoon olive oil
- 1 onion, chopped
- 2 cloves garlic, minced
- 1 cup heavy cream
- 1/2 cup tomato sauce
- 1/2 cup vodka
- 1/4 teaspoon red pepper flakes
- Salt and pepper, to taste
- 1/4 cup grated Parmesan cheese
- Fresh basil leaves, for garnish

Preparation:
1. Cook the penne pasta according to the package instructions. Drain and set aside.
2. In a large skillet, heat the olive oil over medium heat. Add the onion and cook until softened, about 5 minutes.
3. Add the garlic and cook for another minute.
4. Pour in the heavy cream, tomato sauce, vodka, red pepper flakes, salt, and pepper. Stir to combine.
5. Bring the sauce to a boil and then reduce the heat to low. Simmer for about 5 minutes or until the sauce has thickened.
6. Stir in the grated Parmesan cheese.
7. Serve the sauce over the cooked penne pasta and garnish with fresh basil leaves.

Nutrition: Serving size: 1 cup Calories: 572 Fat: 33 g Sodium: 380 mg Carbohydrates: 47 g Protein: 15 g

SPAGHETTI ALLE VONGOLE SPAGHETTI WITH CLAM SAUCE

Cook Time: 20 minutes
Serving: 4
Ingredients:
- 1 pound spaghetti
- 2 tablespoons olive oil
- 4 garlic cloves, minced
- 1/2 teaspoon red pepper flakes
- 2 cups canned clams, drained and chopped
- 1/2 cup dry white wine
- 1/4 cup chopped fresh parsley
- Salt and pepper to taste

Preparation:
1. Cook the spaghetti according to package instructions until al dente. Drain and set aside.
2. In a large skillet, heat the olive oil over medium heat.
3. Add the garlic and red pepper flakes and cook until fragrant, about 1 minute.
4. Add the clams and white wine to the skillet and bring to a simmer.
5. Cook until the wine has reduced by half, about 5 minutes.
6. Stir in the chopped parsley and season with salt and pepper to taste.
7. Toss the cooked spaghetti with the clam sauce in the skillet.
8. Serve hot and garnish with additional parsley if desired.

Nutrition: Serving Size: 1/4 of recipe Calories: 500 Fat: 10g Carbohydrates: 80g Protein: 20g Sodium: 470mg Fiber: 2g.

SPAGHETTI AGLIO OLIO E PEPERONCINO SPAGHETTI WITH GARLIC, OIL, AND HOT PEPPERS

Cook time: 15 minutes
Serving: 2
Ingredients:
- 1 pound spaghetti
- 6 cloves of garlic, minced
- 1/4 cup olive oil
- 1/2 teaspoon red pepper flakes
- Salt to taste
- Freshly ground black pepper to taste
- 1/4 cup chopped fresh parsley leaves
- Parmesan cheese (optional)

Preparation:
1. Cook spaghetti according to the instructions on the package. Reserve 1 cup of pasta water.
2. In a large pan, heat olive oil over medium heat. Add minced garlic and red pepper flakes, cook for 1-2 minutes, until fragrant.
3. Drain the spaghetti and add it to the pan with the garlic and pepper flakes. Toss until the spaghetti is evenly coated with the oil.
4. If the spaghetti seems too dry, add some of the reserved pasta water, 1 tablespoon at a time.
5. Season with salt and freshly ground black pepper to taste.
6. Serve immediately, topped with chopped parsley leaves and grated Parmesan cheese (optional).

Nutrition (per serving): Calories: 700 Fat: 26g Saturated Fat: 4g Cholesterol: 0mg Sodium: 460mg Carbohydrates: 97g Fiber: 5g Sugar: 4g Protein: 18g

TROLI E ALLA GENOVESE PASTA WITH PESTO, GREEN BEANS, AND POTATOES

Cook Time: 30 minutes
Serving: 4
Ingredients:
- 1 lb trofie pasta
- 1 cup Genovese pesto
- 1 lb green beans
- 1 lb potatoes
- Salt and pepper, to taste
- Parmesan cheese, grated, for garnish (optional)

Preparation:
1. Bring a large pot of salted water to a boil. Add the potatoes and cook for 10 minutes, or until they are soft.
2. Add the green beans to the pot and cook for another 5 minutes.
3. Remove the potatoes and green beans from the pot and place them in a serving dish.
4. Add the trofie pasta to the same pot of boiling water and cook according to the package instructions.
5. In a large bowl, mix the pesto with the cooked pasta.

6. Serve the pasta with the potatoes and green beans, and season with salt and pepper, to taste.
7. Garnish with grated Parmesan cheese, if desired.

Nutrition (per serving): Calories: 544 Fat: 28g Carbohydrates: 64g Protein: 13g Fiber: 7g Sodium: 840mg.

TRADITIONAL LASAGNA

Cook time: 1 hour and 30 minutes
Serving: 8
Ingredients:
- 12 lasagna noodles
- 1 pound ground beef
- 1 onion, chopped
- 2 cloves of garlic, minced
- 1 can (28 ounces) crushed tomatoes
- 2 tablespoons tomato paste
- 2 teaspoons dried basil
- 1 teaspoon dried oregano
- 1 teaspoon salt
- 1/2 teaspoon black pepper
- 1 cup ricotta cheese
- 1 egg
- 1/2 cup grated Parmesan cheese
- 2 cups shredded mozzarella cheese
- 1/4 cup chopped fresh parsley (optional)

Preparation:
1. Preheat the oven to 375°F (190°C).
2. Cook the lasagna noodles according to package instructions until al dente. Drain and set aside.
3. In a large skillet over medium heat, cook the ground beef, onion, and garlic until the meat is browned and the onion is tender. Drain any excess grease.
4. Add the crushed tomatoes, tomato paste, basil, oregano, salt, and pepper to the skillet. Stir to combine and let simmer for 10 minutes.
5. In a separate bowl, mix together the ricotta cheese, egg, and Parmesan cheese.
6. Grease a 9x13 inch baking dish and spread a thin layer of the meat sauce on the bottom.
7. Layer 3 lasagna noodles on top of the meat sauce. Spread half of the ricotta cheese mixture on top of the noodles, and sprinkle with 1 cup of mozzarella cheese.
8. Repeat this layering process with 3 more lasagna noodles, the remaining meat sauce, the remaining ricotta cheese mixture, and another cup of mozzarella cheese.
9. Finish with a final layer of 3 lasagna noodles and the remaining mozzarella cheese.
10. Cover the baking dish with foil and bake for 30 minutes. Remove the foil and bake for an additional 15 minutes, or until the cheese is melted and golden brown.
11. Let cool for 10 minutes before serving, garnished with fresh parsley if desired.

Nutrition: Per serving (8 servings): Calories: 460 Fat: 22g Saturated Fat: 12g Cholesterol: 87mg Sodium: 889mg Carbohydrates: 41g Fiber: 4g Sugar: 7g Protein: 25g.

PASTA ALLA NORMA SICILIAN PASTA WITH EGGPLANT SAUCE

Cook time: 25 minutes

Serving: 4-6

Ingredients:
- 1 large eggplant, diced
- 2 medium tomatoes, diced
- 1 medium onion, chopped
- 4 garlic cloves, minced
- 1 tsp dried basil
- 1 tsp dried oregano
- Salt and pepper to taste
- 1 cup olive oil
- 1 lb pasta
- 1 cup grated Pecorino Romano cheese
- Fresh basil leaves, for garnish

Preparation:
1. In a large saucepan, heat the olive oil over medium heat. Add the eggplant, onion, and garlic and cook until the eggplant is soft and the onion is translucent, about 10 minutes.
2. Add the diced tomatoes, basil, oregano, salt, and pepper to the saucepan and continue to cook for another 5 minutes.
3. Cook the pasta according to package instructions until al dente. Reserve 1 cup of the pasta water.
4. Add the cooked pasta to the saucepan with the eggplant sauce and toss to combine. Add some of the reserved pasta water if the sauce is too thick.
5. Serve the pasta with grated Pecorino Romano cheese and fresh basil leaves.

Nutrition (per serving, based on 6 servings): Calories: 450 Fat: 26g Carbohydrates: 42g Protein: 12g Fiber: 4g

POTATO GNOCCHI

Cook time: 20 minutes
Serving: 4-6

Ingredients:
- 2 lbs of potatoes
- 2 cups of all-purpose flour
- 2 eggs
- Salt to taste
- Olive oil
- Parmesan cheese (optional)

Preparation:
1. Boil the potatoes until they are soft and then peel and mash them.
2. In a large bowl, mix the mashed potatoes, flour, eggs, and salt until it forms a smooth dough.
3. Roll the dough into long, thin ropes, about 1 inch in diameter. Cut the ropes into 1-inch pieces.
4. Roll the pieces of dough into a ball and then press down with a fork, making ridges on one side.
5. In a large pot, bring a pot of salted water to a boil and then add the gnocchi.
6. Cook the gnocchi for about 2-3 minutes or until they float to the surface.
7. Remove the gnocchi with a slotted spoon and place in a serving dish.
8. Toss with olive oil and grated Parmesan cheese, if desired.

Nutrition (per serving, based on 6 servings): Calories: 301 Fat: 4 g Saturated Fat: 2 g Cholesterol: 75 mg Sodium: 49 mg Total Carbohydrates: 60 g Dietary Fiber: 4 g Sugars: 2 g Protein: 11 g

GNOCCHI ALLA SORRENTINA

Cook time: 25 minutes
Serving: 4 people
Ingredients:
- 1 lb. gnocchi
- 4 cups tomato sauce
- 1 cup fresh mozzarella cheese, diced
- 1/2 cup grated parmesan cheese
- 1/4 cup fresh basil, chopped
- Salt and pepper to taste
- Olive oil for frying

Preparation:
1. Cook the gnocchi in a large pot of boiling salted water until they float to the surface. Drain and set aside.
2. In a large skillet, heat 2 tablespoons of olive oil over medium heat. Add the tomato sauce and simmer for 5 minutes.
3. Add the cooked gnocchi to the sauce and toss until they are coated.
4. Spread the gnocchi evenly in the skillet and sprinkle the mozzarella and parmesan cheese on top.
5. Place the skillet under the broiler for 2-3 minutes or until the cheese is melted and bubbly.
6. Remove from the oven and sprinkle with fresh basil, salt, and pepper to taste. Serve hot.

Nutrition: Serving size: 1/4 of the recipe Calories: 400 Fat: 19g Saturated Fat: 8g Cholesterol: 37mg Sodium: 727mg Carbohydrates: 42g Fiber: 4g Sugar: 5g Protein: 16g

BIGOI IN SALSA PASTA WITH ANCHOVY SAUCE, VENETIAN STYLE

Cook time: 20 minutes
Serving: 4-6
Ingredients:
- 1 pound bigoi pasta
- 1 can of anchovies in oil
- 2 garlic cloves, minced
- 1/2 teaspoon red pepper flakes
- 1/2 cup olive oil
- 1/2 cup white wine
- 1/2 cup fresh parsley, chopped
- Salt and pepper to taste

Preparation:
1. Cook the bigoi pasta according to package instructions, until al dente. Drain and set aside.
2. In a large saucepan, heat the olive oil over medium heat. Add the minced garlic and red pepper flakes and cook for 1-2 minutes, until fragrant.
3. Add the anchovies to the saucepan, breaking them up with a fork. Cook for 2-3 minutes, until the anchovies have dissolved into the oil.
4. Pour in the white wine and cook for 2-3 minutes, until slightly reduced.
5. Add the cooked bigoi pasta to the saucepan and toss to coat with the anchovy sauce.
6. Sprinkle with fresh parsley and season with salt and pepper to taste. Serve immediately.

Nutrition (per serving, based on 6 servings): Calories: 460 Fat: 29g Protein: 12g Carbohydrates: 40g Fiber: 2g Sugar: 2g

PIZZA AND BREAD

HOMEMADE PIZZA DOUGH

Cook time: 15 minutes (prep time) + 15-20 minutes (baking time)
Serving: 4-6 people
Ingredients:
- 1 cup warm water
- 2 1/4 teaspoons active dry yeast
- 1 teaspoon sugar
- 3 cups all-purpose flour
- 1 teaspoon salt
- 2 tablespoons olive oil

Preparation:
1. In a large mixing bowl, combine the warm water, yeast, and sugar. Stir until the yeast and sugar have dissolved.
2. Let the mixture sit for 5-10 minutes until it becomes frothy.
3. Add in the flour, salt, and olive oil. Mix until the dough forms.
4. Turn the dough onto a floured surface and knead for about 5 minutes until it is smooth and elastic.
5. Place the dough into a greased bowl and cover with a damp cloth. Let it rise for about 30 minutes in a warm place.
6. Preheat the oven to 425°F.
7. Once the dough has risen, punch it down and turn it onto a floured surface.
8. Divide the dough into 4-6 equal parts, depending on the desired size of the pizzas.
9. Roll each part of the dough into a round shape and place it on a greased baking sheet or pizza stone.
10. Add the desired toppings and bake for 15-20 minutes until the crust is golden brown.

Nutrition (per serving based on 6 servings): Calories: 199 Fat: 5g Sodium: 389mg Carbohydrates: 35g Protein: 5g

PIZZA MARGHERITA

Cook time: 15-20 minutes
Serving: 4 people
Ingredients:
- 1/2 teaspoon salt
- 1 teaspoon sugar
- 1/2 teaspoon dry yeast
- 3 cups all-purpose flour
- 1/2 cup warm water
- 1/2 cup tomato sauce
- 1 cup shredded mozzarella cheese
- 1/4 cup grated Parmesan cheese
- 1/4 cup chopped fresh basil
- 4 tablespoons olive oil
- Salt and pepper to taste

Preparation:

1. In a large mixing bowl, combine the salt, sugar, and yeast.
2. Add the flour and warm water to the bowl and mix until it forms a dough.
3. Knead the dough for 5-7 minutes, then cover it and let it rest for 10 minutes.
4. Preheat the oven to 425°F.
5. Roll out the dough on a floured surface to form a 12-inch circle.
6. Place the dough on a greased baking sheet or pizza stone.
7. Brush the dough with olive oil and spread the tomato sauce over the top.
8. Sprinkle the mozzarella cheese and Parmesan cheese over the sauce.
9. Add salt and pepper to taste.
10. Bake the pizza for 15-20 minutes, or until the crust is crispy and the cheese is melted.
11. Remove from the oven and sprinkle the chopped basil over the top.

Nutrition (per serving): Calories: 309 Fat: 16 g Protein: 13 g Carbohydrates: 27 g Fiber: 2 g Sugar: 2 g Sodium: 563 mg

PIZZA WITH BURRATA CHEESE AND FRESH TOMATOES

Cook time: 20-25 minutes
Serving: 4 servings
Ingredients:
- 1 pre-made pizza crust
- 2 cups of burrata cheese
- 2 cups of fresh cherry tomatoes, halved
- 1 tablespoon of olive oil
- Salt and pepper to taste
- Fresh basil leaves for garnish

Preparation:
1. Preheat oven to 425°F (220°C).
2. Place the pizza crust on a baking sheet or pizza stone.
3. Spread the burrata cheese evenly over the pizza crust, leaving a 1-inch border.
4. Add the halved cherry tomatoes on top of the cheese.
5. Drizzle olive oil over the tomatoes and sprinkle with salt and pepper.
6. Bake in the oven for 20-25 minutes or until the crust is crispy and golden brown.
7. Remove from oven and garnish with fresh basil leaves.
8. Serve hot and enjoy!

Nutrition (per serving): Calories: 361 Fat: 25g Carbohydrates: 28g Protein: 14g Sodium: 864mg

PANZEROTTI FRIED STUFFED PIZZA

Cook time: 15-20 minutes
Serving: 4-6
Ingredients:
- 1 package of pizza dough
- 1 cup of mozzarella cheese, grated
- 1/2 cup of tomato sauce
- 1/4 cup of chopped pepperoni
- 1/4 cup of diced onion
- 1/4 cup of diced green bell pepper

- 1/4 cup of sliced black olives
- 1/4 cup of chopped basil
- 1 tablespoon of olive oil
- Salt and pepper to taste
- Flour for dusting

Preparation:
1. Preheat the oven to 400°F (200°C).
2. In a pan, heat the olive oil over medium heat. Add the diced onion and green bell pepper and cook until softened.
3. In a mixing bowl, combine the grated mozzarella cheese, cooked onions and peppers, pepperoni, black olives, and chopped basil. Mix well.
4. Dust a clean surface with flour and roll out the pizza dough into a circle. Cut the dough into 4-6 equal pieces.
5. Spoon about 2 tablespoons of the cheese mixture onto each piece of dough. Roll the edges of the dough over the cheese mixture, making a crescent shape.
6. Place the panzerotti on a baking sheet lined with parchment paper. Bake in the oven for 15-20 minutes, or until the dough is golden brown and the cheese is melted.
7. Serve hot with tomato sauce on the side.

Nutrition (per serving): Calories: 300 Fat: 12 g Protein: 12 g Carbohydrates: 36 g Sodium: 860 mg

GNOCCO FRITTO FRIED HOMEMADE BREAD

Cook Time: 20 minutes
Serving: 4-6 portions
Ingredients:
- 500 g of all-purpose flour
- 200 ml of warm water
- 20 g of fresh yeast
- 10 g of salt
- 2 tablespoons of extra virgin olive oil
- Vegetable oil for frying

Preparation:
1. In a large mixing bowl, combine the warm water and yeast. Stir until the yeast is dissolved.
2. Add the flour, salt, and olive oil to the yeast mixture. Mix until a soft dough is formed.
3. Knead the dough for about 10 minutes until it is smooth and elastic.
4. Place the dough in a greased bowl and cover with plastic wrap. Allow the dough to rise in a warm place for about 1 hour or until it has doubled in size.
5. Roll out the dough to a thickness of about 1 cm. Cut the dough into square pieces, about 4 cm wide.
6. Heat the vegetable oil in a frying pan over medium heat.
7. Fry the pieces of dough in the oil until they are golden brown, about 2 minutes on each side.
8. Remove the gnocco fritto from the oil and drain on paper towels. Serve warm.

Nutrition: (per serving) Calories: 300 Kcal Total Fat: 15 g Saturated Fat: 1.5 g Cholesterol: 0 mg Sodium: 810 mg Total Carbohydrates: 36 g Dietary Fiber: 2 g Sugar: 1 g Protein: 7 g

ROSEMARY FOCACCIA BREAD

Cook Time: 25-30 minutes
Serving: 8-10 slices
Ingredients:
- 2 1/2 cups all-purpose flour
- 1 tsp instant yeast
- 2 tsp salt
- 1 tsp sugar
- 1 1/2 tbsp fresh rosemary, chopped
- 2 tbsp olive oil
- 1 1/4 cups warm water
- Cornmeal for dusting

Preparation:
1. In a large bowl, mix the flour, yeast, salt, sugar, and rosemary.
2. Add the olive oil and warm water, and mix until a dough forms.
3. Knead the dough on a floured surface for 10 minutes until smooth and elastic.
4. Place the dough in a lightly oiled bowl, cover, and let it rise for 1 hour.
5. Preheat your oven to 425°F.
6. Dust a baking sheet with cornmeal and transfer the dough onto the sheet.
7. Make indentations on the surface of the dough using your fingers and brush with more olive oil.
8. Bake for 25-30 minutes, or until the top is golden brown.
9. Remove from the oven and let it cool for 10 minutes.

Nutrition (per slice, based on 10 slices): Calories: 164 Fat: 5 g Saturated Fat: 1 g Carbohydrates: 26 g Protein: 4 g Sugar: 2 g Sodium: 503 mg

FOCACCIA BREAD WITH CHERRY TOMATOES

Cook time: 20 minutes
Serving: 8 slices
Ingredients:
- 1 cup all-purpose flour
- 1 1/2 cups bread flour
- 1 1/2 teaspoons salt
- 2 teaspoons sugar
- 1 1/2 teaspoons active dry yeast
- 1/2 cup warm water
- 1/2 cup olive oil
- 1 cup cherry tomatoes, halved
- Coarse salt for sprinkling on top
- Fresh basil leaves for garnish (optional)

Preparation:
1. In a large bowl, mix together both flours, salt, and sugar.
2. In a separate bowl, mix together the yeast and warm water. Let sit for 5 minutes, or until frothy.
3. Pour the yeast mixture into the dry ingredients and mix until a dough forms.
4. Knead the dough on a floured surface for 10 minutes.
5. Place the dough in a lightly oiled bowl, cover with plastic wrap, and let rise for an hour.
6. Preheat your oven to 450°F.
7. On a floured surface, roll the dough out into a large circle. Place the dough on a baking sheet lined with parchment paper.

8. Make dimples in the dough using your fingers. Drizzle olive oil over the top, then place the halved cherry tomatoes on top. Sprinkle coarse salt over the top.
9. Bake for 20 minutes, or until the bread is golden brown.
10. Serve warm with fresh basil leaves as garnish (optional).

Nutrition (per slice, based on 8 slices): Calories: 181 Fat: 11g Saturated Fat: 1.5g Cholesterol: 0mg Sodium: 438mg Carbohydrates: 18g Fiber: 1g Sugar: 1g Protein: 4g

GARLIC ROLLS

Cook time: 25 minutes
Serving: 12 garlic rolls
Ingredients:
- 12 dinner rolls
- 1/2 cup unsalted butter
- 2 cloves garlic, minced
- 1 teaspoon dried basil
- 1/4 teaspoon salt
- 1/4 teaspoon black pepper

Preparation:
1. Preheat oven to 375°F.
2. Cut dinner rolls in half and place the cut side up in a baking dish.
3. In a small saucepan, melt butter over medium heat. Add garlic, dried basil, salt, and black pepper. Stir well.
4. Brush the garlic butter mixture on the cut side of each dinner roll.
5. Bake for 25 minutes or until the rolls are golden brown.
6. Serve hot and enjoy!

Nutrition: Per serving (1 garlic roll): Calories: 210 Fat: 12g Sodium: 410mg Carbohydrates: 23g Protein: 4g

CIABATTA BREAD

Cook time: 35 minutes
Serving: Makes 12 slices
Ingredients:
- 2 cups all-purpose flour
- 1 1/2 cups warm water
- 1 tsp salt
- 1 1/2 tsp active dry yeast
- 2 tbsp olive oil

Preparation:
1. In a large bowl, combine the flour, yeast, and salt. Mix well.
2. Add in the warm water and olive oil and mix until a sticky dough forms.
3. Cover the bowl with plastic wrap and let the dough rest in a warm place for 30 minutes.
4. Preheat your oven to 450°F. Place a baking sheet on the middle rack to preheat.
5. Once the dough has risen, transfer it to a lightly floured surface and shape into a rough rectangle.
6. Transfer the shaped dough to the preheated baking sheet and sprinkle with flour.
7. Bake for 30-35 minutes, or until the bread is golden brown.
8. Remove from the oven and let cool for 10 minutes before slicing and serving.

Nutrition: (Per slice, based on 12 slices) Calories: 120 Fat: 4g Protein: 3g Carbohydrates: 19g Fiber: 1g Sodium: 180mg.

PANE RUSTICO PUGLIESE RUSTIC BREAD LOAF

Cook time: 30-35 minutes
Serving: 1 Loaf (10-12 slices)
Ingredients:
- 500g (17.6 oz) all-purpose flour
- 10g (0.35 oz) salt
- 10g (0.35 oz) sugar
- 7g (0.25 oz) active dry yeast
- 300ml (10.1 oz) lukewarm water
- olive oil for brushing

Preparation:
1. In a large bowl, mix together the flour, salt, sugar, and yeast.
2. Slowly pour in the lukewarm water, mixing until a dough forms.
3. Knead the dough for about 10 minutes until it is smooth and elastic.
4. Place the dough in a greased bowl, cover with plastic wrap and let it rise for about an hour in a warm place.
5. Preheat the oven to 220°C (428°F).
6. Once the dough has risen, transfer it to a greased baking sheet or baking stone.
7. Brush the top of the dough with olive oil.
8. Bake for 30-35 minutes or until the crust is golden brown.
9. Remove from the oven and let it cool on a wire rack before slicing and serving.

Nutrition: Per 1 slice (Based on 12 slices per loaf) Calories: 132 Fat: 1.3g Carbs: 28g Protein: 4.5g Fiber: 1.5g

MEAT AND POULTRY

SALTIMBOCCA ALLA ROMANA ROMAN-STYLE VEAL SCALOPPINE

Cook time: 25 minutes
Serving: 4 people
Ingredients:
- 4 veal scaloppine, pounded thin
- 4 thin slices of prosciutto
- 8 fresh sage leaves
- 1/2 cup all-purpose flour
- Salt and pepper, to taste
- 2 tablespoons olive oil
- 1/2 cup white wine
- 1/2 cup chicken broth
- 1 tablespoon unsalted butter

Preparation:
1. Place a sage leaf and a slice of prosciutto on top of each veal scaloppine.

2. Secure the prosciutto and sage to the veal with toothpicks or kitchen twine.
3. Dredge each veal scaloppine in flour, seasoned with salt and pepper.
4. Heat the olive oil in a large skillet over medium-high heat.
5. Cook the veal scaloppine for 2-3 minutes on each side, until browned.
6. Remove the veal scaloppine from the skillet and set aside.
7. Add the wine to the same skillet, scraping up any browned bits from the bottom of the pan.
8. Let the wine reduce by half.
9. Add the chicken broth to the skillet and let it reduce by half.
10. Stir in the butter until melted and fully combined.
11. Return the veal scaloppine to the skillet and cook for an additional minute on each side, until heated through.
12. Serve the veal scaloppine hot with the sauce spooned over the top.

Nutrition: Servings: 4 Calories: 384 Total Fat: 24g Saturated Fat: 8g Cholesterol: 112mgSodium: 756mg Total Carbohydrates: 15g Dietary Fiber: 1g Sugar: 1g Protein: 26g.

OSSOBUCHI ALLA MILANESE MILANESE-STYLE VEAL SHANK

Cook Time: 2 hours
Serving: 4-6 people
Ingredients:
- 4 veal shanks (ossobuchi)
- 2 cups of breadcrumbs
- 1 cup of grated Parmesan cheese
- 2 eggs, lightly beaten
- 2 tablespoons of olive oil
- 4 cloves of garlic, minced
- 1 large onion, chopped
- 2 cups of chicken or beef broth
- 1 cup of white wine
- 2 tablespoons of tomato paste
- Salt and pepper, to taste
- Fresh parsley, chopped (for garnish)

Preparation:
1. Preheat oven to 375°F.
2. In a shallow dish, mix breadcrumbs and Parmesan cheese.
3. In another shallow dish, beat the eggs.
4. Season the veal shanks with salt and pepper.
5. Dip each veal shank into the beaten eggs, then coat with the breadcrumb mixture.
6. In a large skillet, heat the olive oil over medium heat.
7. Brown the veal shanks in the skillet for 3-4 minutes on each side, until golden.
8. Transfer the veal shanks to a baking dish.
9. In the same skillet, add the garlic and onion. Cook until soft and fragrant, about 5 minutes.
10. Add the broth, white wine, and tomato paste to the skillet. Stir until well combined.
11. Pour the mixture over the veal shanks in the baking dish.
12. Cover the baking dish with foil and place in the oven. Bake for 2 hours, or until the meat is tender and falling off the bone.
13. Serve the ossobuchi alla Milanese with mashed potatoes, polenta, or risotto. Garnish with fresh parsley.

Nutrition: Per serving (based on 6 servings): Calories: 551 Fat: 26g Saturated Fat: 8g Cholesterol: 168mg Sodium: 921mg Carbohydrates: 34g Fiber: 2g Sugar: 5g Protein: 46g

POLLO ALLA CACCIATORA HUNTER'S CHICKEN STEW

Cook time: 45 minutes
Serving: 4-6 people
Ingredients:
- 4 chicken legs and thighs, skin removed
- 2 tbsp olive oil
- 1 onion, chopped
- 3 garlic cloves, minced
- 1 cup red wine
- 1 can diced tomatoes (14.5 oz)
- 1 cup chicken broth
- 1 tbsp dried thyme
- 1 tsp dried rosemary
- 1 tsp dried oregano
- Salt and pepper to taste
- 2 tbsp cornstarch mixed with 2 tbsp water (optional)
- Fresh parsley, chopped (optional)

Preparation:
1. Heat the olive oil in a large pot or Dutch oven over medium heat.
2. Add the chicken and cook until brown on both sides, about 5 minutes per side.
3. Remove the chicken from the pot and set aside.
4. Add the onion and garlic to the pot and cook until softened, about 5 minutes.
5. Pour in the red wine and stir, scraping the bottom of the pot to release any browned bits.
6. Add the diced tomatoes, chicken broth, thyme, rosemary, oregano, salt, and pepper. Stir to combine.
7. Return the chicken to the pot and bring the mixture to a simmer.
8. Reduce heat to low, cover, and cook for 30 minutes, or until the chicken is fully cooked.
9. If the stew is too thin, remove the chicken and whisk in the cornstarch mixture until thickened.
10. Return the chicken to the pot and serve with fresh parsley, if desired.

Nutrition (per serving): Calories: 409 Fat: 23.2g Carbs: 11.3g Protein: 38.4g Fiber: 2.4g

POLPETTE AL SUGO MEATBALLS IN TOMATO SAUCE

Cook time: 25-30 minutes
Serving: 4
Ingredients:
- 1 lb ground beef
- 1 egg
- 1/2 cup breadcrumbs
- 1/4 cup grated Parmesan cheese
- 1 tsp minced garlic
- 1 tsp dried basil
- 1 tsp dried oregano

- Salt and pepper to taste
- 1 can of crushed tomatoes (28 oz)
- 2 tbsp olive oil
- 1 medium onion, chopped
- 2 cloves garlic, minced
- Salt and pepper to taste

Preparation:
1. In a large mixing bowl, combine ground beef, egg, breadcrumbs, Parmesan cheese, 1 tsp minced garlic, dried basil, dried oregano, salt, and pepper. Mix well until all ingredients are well combined.
2. Using your hands, form mixture into golf ball-sized meatballs and set aside.
3. In a large saucepan, heat 2 tbsp of olive oil over medium heat. Add chopped onion and 2 cloves of minced garlic and sauté until softened, about 5 minutes.
4. Add the can of crushed tomatoes and salt and pepper to taste. Bring the sauce to a simmer.
5. Place the meatballs into the sauce and let cook for 20-25 minutes, or until the meatballs are cooked through.
6. Serve with a side of pasta or your favorite bread.

Nutrition: (per serving, based on 4 servings) Calories: 468 Total Fat: 26g Saturated Fat: 9g Cholesterol: 138mg Sodium: 531mg Total Carbohydrates: 17g Dietary Fiber: 2g Protein: 41g

POLPETTE FRITTE FRIED MEATBALLS

Cook time: 25 minutes
Serving: 4
Ingredients:
- 1 lb ground beef
- 1 egg
- 1/2 cup breadcrumbs
- 1/4 cup grated parmesan cheese
- 1 clove garlic, minced
- 1 tsp dried basil
- 1 tsp dried oregano
- Salt and pepper to taste
- Oil for frying

Preparation:
1. In a large bowl, combine the ground beef, egg, breadcrumbs, parmesan cheese, garlic, basil, oregano, salt, and pepper. Mix until well combined.
2. Shape the mixture into golf-ball sized meatballs.
3. Heat the oil in a large frying pan over medium-high heat.
4. Fry the meatballs in the hot oil, turning occasionally, until they are browned on all sides and cooked through, about 8-10 minutes.
5. Remove the meatballs from the pan with a slotted spoon and drain on paper towels.
6. Serve with your favorite dipping sauce.

Nutrition:
Per serving: 400 calories, 24g fat, 22g protein, 20g carbohydrates, 2g fiber, 6g sugar.

COTOLETTA ALLA MILANESE MILANESE-STYLE VEAL CHOP

Cook time: 20-25 minutes
Serving: 2 people
Ingredients:

- 2 veal chops, about 1 inch thick
- 2 large eggs
- 1 cup breadcrumbs
- 1/2 cup grated Parmesan cheese
- Salt and pepper to taste
- 1/4 cup flour
- 1/2 cup olive oil

Preparation:

1. Start by pounding the veal chops to a thickness of 1/4 inch.
2. Season the veal chops with salt and pepper.
3. In a shallow dish, beat the eggs and add salt and pepper to taste.
4. In another shallow dish, mix together the breadcrumbs and Parmesan cheese.
5. Place the flour in a third shallow dish.
6. Dip each veal chop first in the flour, then in the eggs, and finally in the breadcrumb mixture.
7. Heat the olive oil in a large frying pan over medium heat.
8. Add the veal chops to the pan and cook for about 5 minutes on each side, until golden brown.
9. Serve hot with a lemon wedge and your favorite side dish.

Nutrition: 1 serving (1 veal chop) contains approximately: 450 calories 32g protein 20g fat 25g carbohydrates

BRASATO AL BAROLO BEEF STEW BRAISED IN BAROLO WINE

Cook time: 3 hours
Serving: 4-6 people
Ingredients:

- 2 lbs beef (chuck roast or short ribs)
- 2 tbsp olive oil
- 2 onions, diced
- 3 carrots, peeled and diced
- 3 celery stalks, diced
- 4 garlic cloves, minced
- 1 cup Barolo wine
- 2 cups beef broth
- 2 tbsp tomato paste
- 2 tbsp chopped fresh rosemary
- 2 tbsp chopped fresh thyme
- 2 bay leaves
- Salt and pepper to taste

Preparation:

1. Heat the olive oil in a large Dutch oven over medium heat.
2. Season the beef with salt and pepper and brown it on all sides. Remove the beef and set it aside.
3. Add the onions, carrots, and celery to the Dutch oven and cook until softened, about 5-7 minutes.

4. Add the garlic and cook for another minute.
5. Pour in the Barolo wine and stir to scrape up any browned bits from the bottom of the pot.
6. Add the beef broth, tomato paste, rosemary, thyme, and bay leaves. Stir to combine.
7. Return the beef to the pot, cover, and bring to a simmer.
8. Reduce heat to low and let it simmer for 2-3 hours, or until the beef is tender.
9. Season with salt and pepper to taste. Serve with mashed potatoes or crusty bread.

Nutrition (per serving, based on 6 servings): Calories: 435 Total Fat: 22 g Saturated Fat: 8 g Cholesterol: 153 mg Sodium: 534 mg Total Carbohydrates: 10 g Dietary Fiber: 2 g Sugar: 4 g Protein: 47 g

SCALOPPINE AL MARSALA CON FUNGHI MARSALA SCALOPPINE WITH MUSHROOMS

Cook time: 25-30 minutes
Serving: 4
Ingredients:
- 4 veal scaloppine cutlets
- 1 cup all-purpose flour
- Salt and pepper, to taste
- 4 tablespoons unsalted butter
- 1/2 cup sliced mushrooms
- 1/2 cup Marsala wine
- 1/2 cup beef broth
- 1/4 teaspoon dried thyme
- 2 tablespoons minced shallots

Preparation:
1. Season the flour with salt and pepper and place it in a shallow dish.
2. Dredge the veal cutlets in the seasoned flour, shaking off any excess.
3. In a large skillet, heat 2 tablespoons of butter over medium-high heat.
4. Add the veal cutlets to the skillet and cook for 3-4 minutes on each side until golden brown.
5. Remove the veal from the skillet and set it aside on a plate.
6. In the same skillet, add the remaining butter and sauté the sliced mushrooms for 2-3 minutes.
7. Add the minced shallots to the skillet and sauté for another minute.
8. Pour in the Marsala wine and the beef broth and stir well.
9. Add the dried thyme and bring the mixture to a simmer.
10. Return the veal cutlets to the skillet and simmer for 5-7 minutes until the sauce has thickened and the veal is cooked through.

Nutrition: Serving size: 1 veal cutlet with sauce Calories: 365 Fat: 18g Saturated fat: 11g Carbohydrates: 16g Protein: 33g Sodium: 383mg

COSCE D'ANATRA BRASATE BRAISED DUCK LEGS

Cook time: 2 hours
Serving: 4
Ingredients:
- 4 duck legs
- 4 cloves of garlic, minced
- 2 tablespoons of olive oil
- 1 onion, chopped

- 2 carrots, chopped
- 2 celery stalks, chopped
- 2 cups of red wine
- 2 cups of chicken or duck broth
- 1 teaspoon of dried thyme
- Salt and pepper to taste

Preparation:
1. Preheat oven to 350°F (175°C).
2. In a large skillet, heat the olive oil over medium heat.
3. Add the duck legs and cook until they are browned on all sides.
4. Remove the duck legs from the pan and set aside.
5. Add the garlic, onion, carrots, and celery to the same pan and cook until softened.
6. Return the duck legs to the pan, add the red wine, chicken or duck broth, thyme, salt and pepper.
7. Bring the mixture to a boil and then transfer the pan to the preheated oven.
8. Bake the duck legs for 1 hour, or until they are tender and the sauce has reduced.
9. Serve the duck legs with the sauce on the side.

Nutrition: Per serving (based on 4 servings): Calories: 600 Fat: 41g Carbohydrates: 9g Protein: 49g Sodium: 564mg Cholesterol: 184mg.

SCOTTADITO ALLA ROMANA ROMAN-STYLE GRILLED LAMB CHOPS

Cook time: 20 minutes
Serving: 4
Ingredients:
- 8 lamb chops
- 1/4 cup extra virgin olive oil
- 2 garlic cloves, minced
- 1 lemon, zested and juiced
- 2 teaspoons dried oregano
- 1 teaspoon dried rosemary
- 1 teaspoon salt
- 1/2 teaspoon black pepper

Preparation:
1. In a large bowl, mix together olive oil, minced garlic, lemon zest, lemon juice, dried oregano, dried rosemary, salt, and black pepper.
2. Add the lamb chops to the bowl and marinate for at least 30 minutes.
3. Preheat the grill to high heat.
4. Remove the lamb chops from the marinade and place on the hot grill.
5. Cook the lamb chops for 4-5 minutes on each side, or until they reach an internal temperature of 145°F.
6. Serve with lemon wedges and additional salt, if desired.

Nutrition:
Per serving: 400 calories, 33g fat, 1g carbohydrates, 25g protein.

BRASATO DI MAIALE ALLA BIRRA BEER-BRAISED PORK STEW

Cook Time: 2 hours and 30 minutes

Serving: 6 portions
Ingredients:
- 1 kilogram of pork shoulder, cut into 2-inch cubes
- 3 tablespoons of olive oil
- 2 onions, diced
- 4 garlic cloves, minced
- 2 tablespoons of tomato paste
- 1 cup of dark beer
- 1 cup of chicken broth
- 2 bay leaves
- 2 sprigs of rosemary
- 1 tablespoon of dried thyme
- Salt and pepper to taste
- 2 tablespoons of cornstarch
- 2 tablespoons of cold water

Preparation:
1. Heat the olive oil in a large pot over medium heat.
2. Add the pork cubes and cook until browned on all sides.
3. Remove the pork from the pot and set aside.
4. In the same pot, add the onions and garlic and cook until they are softened.
5. Add the tomato paste and stir to combine.
6. Pour in the beer, chicken broth, bay leaves, rosemary, thyme, salt, and pepper.
7. Return the pork to the pot, cover, and simmer for 2 hours.
8. In a small bowl, mix the cornstarch and water.
9. Stir the mixture into the stew and cook for an additional 10 minutes.
10. Serve hot with crusty bread or mashed potatoes.

Nutrition: Per serving: Calories: 442 Fat: 25 g Carbohydrates: 8 g Protein: 45 g Sodium: 368 mg Fiber: 1 g.

SPEZZATTINO DI POLLO ALL'ARRABBIATA CHICKEN STEW ALL'ARRABBIATA

Cook time: 1 hour
Serving: 4
Ingredients:
- 1 lb boneless chicken breast, cut into bite-sized pieces
- 1 onion, chopped
- 4 cloves of garlic, minced
- 2 tablespoons olive oil
- 1 can (28 oz) of crushed tomatoes
- 1 teaspoon dried oregano
- 1 teaspoon red pepper flakes
- 1 cup chicken broth
- Salt and pepper to taste
- Fresh basil leaves for garnish

Preparation:
1. In a large saucepan, heat the olive oil over medium heat.
2. Add the chopped onion and minced garlic, cook until softened and fragrant, about 3 minutes.
3. Add the chicken pieces to the pan and cook until browned on all sides.

4. Pour in the crushed tomatoes, chicken broth, dried oregano, red pepper flakes, salt, and pepper. Stir to combine.
5. Bring the mixture to a boil, then reduce heat to low and let it simmer for 45 minutes.
6. Stir occasionally until the sauce has thickened and the chicken is cooked through.
7. Serve the chicken stew hot, garnished with fresh basil leaves.

Nutrition: (per serving) Calories: 270 Total Fat: 12g Saturated Fat: 2g Cholesterol: 73mg Sodium: 530mg Total Carbohydrates: 12g Dietary Fiber: 3g Sugars: 6g Protein: 29g

FISH AND SEAFOOD

INSALATA DI POLPO E PATATE OCTOPUS AND POTATO SALAD

Cook time: 20 minutes
Serving: 4
Ingredients:
- 1 lb octopus, cleaned and sliced into bite-sized pieces
- 2 medium sized potatoes, peeled and diced
- 1 red onion, diced
- 1 red pepper, diced
- 1/4 cup of extra virgin olive oil
- 3 tablespoons of white wine vinegar
- Salt and pepper, to taste
- A handful of parsley, chopped

Preparation:
1. In a medium sized pot, boil the octopus and potatoes until they are tender (around 10-15 minutes).
2. In a bowl, mix the olive oil and white wine vinegar together. Season with salt and pepper to taste.
3. Once the octopus and potatoes are cooked, drain and let them cool to room temperature.
4. In a large bowl, combine the octopus, potatoes, red onion, red pepper, and parsley.
5. Pour the olive oil and white wine vinegar mixture over the top of the octopus and potato mixture and mix until evenly coated.
6. Serve chilled and enjoy!

Nutrition: Per serving: Calories: 325 Fat: 19 g Protein: 21 g Carbohydrates: 22 g Fiber: 2 g Sodium: 11 mg

POLPO ALLA GRIGLIA GRILLED OCTOPUS WITH VEGETABLES

Cook time: 25 minutes
Serving: 4 people
Ingredients:
- 1 large octopus (about 1 kg)
- 4 large potatoes
- 2 medium zucchinis
- 1 red bell pepper
- 1 yellow bell pepper
- 1 large red onion
- 6 cloves of garlic
- 1 lemon
- 4 tablespoons of olive oil
- Salt
- Fresh parsley
- Balsamic vinegar (optional)

Preparation:
1. Clean the octopus by removing the beak, eyes, and the inside of the head. Cut the tentacles into 4-5 pieces.
2. Boil the octopus in a pot of water with 2 cloves of garlic, lemon juice, and salt for about 20 minutes or until tender.

3. Cut the vegetables into large pieces and place in a large bowl.
4. Drizzle with olive oil, salt, and freshly squeezed lemon juice. Mix well.
5. Grill the octopus and vegetables on a hot grill for 5-7 minutes, turning occasionally.
6. Place the grilled vegetables on a serving dish and top with the grilled octopus.
7. Sprinkle with fresh parsley and a drizzle of balsamic vinegar (optional).

Nutrition: Serving size: 1 serving (without balsamic vinegar) Calories: 334 Fat: 17g Saturated fat: 2g Cholesterol: 51mg Sodium: 494mg Carbohydrates: 24g Fiber: 4g Sugar: 4g Protein: 20g

CALAMARI RIPIENI STUFFED CALAMARI

Cook time: 30 minutes
Serving: 4
Ingredients:
- 8 large calamari tubes
- 1 cup cooked rice
- 1/2 cup chopped tomato
- 1/2 cup chopped onion
- 1/2 cup chopped green pepper
- 2 cloves garlic, minced
- 1/4 cup chopped fresh parsley
- 2 tablespoons olive oil
- 1 tablespoon lemon juice
- Salt and pepper to taste
- 1/2 cup bread crumbs
- 1/2 cup grated Parmesan cheese
- 1 egg, lightly beaten
- 2 cups tomato sauce

Preparation:
1. Preheat the oven to 375°F.
2. Clean the calamari tubes and cut the tentacles into small pieces.
3. In a large bowl, mix together the cooked rice, chopped tomato, onion, green pepper, garlic, parsley, olive oil, lemon juice, salt and pepper.
4. Stir in the bread crumbs, Parmesan cheese, egg, and chopped tentacles.
5. Spoon the mixture into the calamari tubes, filling each one about 3/4 full.
6. Place the stuffed calamari in a baking dish and pour the tomato sauce over them.
7. Bake in the oven for 25-30 minutes, or until the calamari are tender and the filling is lightly browned.
8. Serve hot with a side of crusty bread.

Nutrition: (per serving) Calories: 334 Fat: 15g Protein: 25g Carbohydrates: 26g Fiber: 2g Sugar: 6g Sodium: 853mg

COZZE GRATINATE PUGLIESI BAKED STUFFED MUSSELS

Cook time: 30 minutes
Serving: 4-6
Ingredients:
- 24 mussels, scrubbed and de-bearded

- 1/2 cup breadcrumbs
- 2 cloves garlic, minced
- 2 tablespoons chopped fresh parsley
- 2 tablespoons chopped fresh basil
- 1/4 cup grated Parmesan cheese
- 1/4 cup extra-virgin olive oil
- Salt and pepper to taste

Preparation:
1. Preheat the oven to 400°F.
2. In a mixing bowl, combine the breadcrumbs, garlic, parsley, basil, Parmesan cheese, olive oil, salt, and pepper.
3. Stuff each mussel with the breadcrumb mixture, then arrange the mussels in a baking dish.
4. Bake the mussels for 25-30 minutes or until golden brown and crispy.
5. Serve hot with a side of crusty bread.

Nutrition (per serving, based on 6 servings): Calories: 242 Fat: 17.6g Saturated Fat: 3.2g Cholesterol: 28mg Sodium: 572mg Carbohydrates: 14.3g Fiber: 2.1g Sugar: 1.4g Protein: 11.4g

SOGLIOLA ALLA MUGNAIA SAUTÉED DOVER SOLE WITH LEMON

Cook Time: 15 minutes
Serving: 2 people
Ingredients:
- 2 large Dover Sole fillets
- 4 tablespoons of butter
- 2 large lemons, sliced
- Salt and pepper, to taste
- 3 tablespoons of olive oil
- 1 tablespoon of chopped fresh parsley
- 1 tablespoon of chopped fresh basil

Preparation:
1. Rinse the Dover Sole fillets and pat them dry.
2. In a large frying pan, heat the olive oil over medium heat.
3. Season the fillets with salt and pepper and place them in the pan, skin-side down.
4. Cook the fillets for 4-5 minutes on each side or until they are golden brown and crispy.
5. Remove the fillets from the pan and set them aside.
6. In the same pan, add the butter, sliced lemons, and chopped herbs. Cook until the lemon slices are softened and the herbs are fragrant, about 2-3 minutes.
7. Place the cooked fillets back into the pan and baste them with the lemon sauce.
8. Cook for another minute on each side or until the fillets are cooked through.
9. Serve the Sogliola alla Mugnaia with a side of rice, potatoes, or vegetables.

Nutrition: Serving size: 1 fillet (6 oz) Calories: 400 Fat: 32 g Protein: 27 g Carbohydrates: 6 g Sodium: 583 mg Cholesterol: 170 mg

ZUPPA DI PESCE FISH STEW

Cook time: 30 minutes
Serving: 4 people

Ingredients:
- 1 onion, diced
- 2 cloves of garlic, minced
- 1 cup of diced tomatoes
- 1 cup of white wine
- 1 lb of mixed seafood (shrimp, scallops, and fish)
- 4 cups of fish or chicken broth
- 1 tbsp of dried basil
- Salt and pepper to taste
- 1 tbsp of olive oil

Preparation:
1. Heat a large pot over medium heat and add the olive oil.
2. Sauté the onions until they are translucent, about 3 minutes.
3. Add the garlic and cook for another minute.
4. Add the diced tomatoes, wine, broth, and basil to the pot.
5. Bring the mixture to a boil and then reduce the heat to a simmer.
6. Add the seafood to the pot and let it cook for about 10 minutes, or until the seafood is cooked through.
7. Season with salt and pepper to taste.
8. Serve hot in bowls with crusty bread.

Nutrition (per serving): Calories: 360 Fat: 11g Protein: 38g Carbohydrates: 15g Fiber: 2g Sugar: 4g Sodium: 1010mg.

PESCE SPADA ALLA SICILIANA SICILIAN-STYLE SWORDFISH

Cook time: 20 minutes
Serving: 4 people
Ingredients:
- 4 swordfish steaks (6-8 ounces each)
- 1/2 cup olive oil
- 4 cloves garlic, minced
- 1/2 teaspoon salt
- 1/2 teaspoon black pepper
- 1 lemon, sliced
- 1/2 cup diced tomatoes
- 1/4 cup pitted black olives
- 1 tablespoon capers
- 1/4 cup fresh parsley, chopped

Preparation:
1. In a small bowl, mix together the olive oil, garlic, salt, and black pepper.
2. In a large skillet, heat the olive oil mixture over medium-high heat.
3. Add the swordfish steaks and cook for about 4 minutes on each side, or until the fish is cooked through and golden brown.
4. Remove the swordfish from the skillet and place it on a serving platter.
5. In the same skillet, add the lemon slices and cook for 2 minutes on each side.
6. Add the diced tomatoes, olives, capers, and parsley to the skillet. Cook for 2-3 minutes, until the ingredients are heated through.
7. Pour the tomato mixture over the swordfish steaks and serve hot.

Nutrition: Serving size: 1 swordfish steak Calories: 305 Fat: 22 g Protein: 28 g Carbohydrates: 4 g Sodium: 666 mg Cholesterol: 83 mg

FILETTI DI DENTICE AL CARTOCCIO RED SNAPPER FILLETS BAKED IN FOIL

Cook Time: 25 minutes

Serving: 4 portions

Ingredients:
- 4 red snapper fillets, about 6 ounces each
- 4 cloves of garlic, minced
- 1 lemon, sliced
- 4 tablespoons of olive oil
- 1 teaspoon of dried basil
- 1 teaspoon of dried oregano
- Salt and pepper to taste
- 4 tablespoons of white wine
- 4 tablespoons of butter, cut into small pieces
- 4 sheets of aluminum foil

Preparation:
1. Preheat the oven to 375°F.
2. Place each red snapper fillet on a sheet of aluminum foil.
3. Sprinkle the minced garlic over each fillet.
4. Arrange the lemon slices on top of the fillets.
5. Drizzle each fillet with 1 tablespoon of olive oil.
6. Sprinkle the dried basil and oregano over each fillet.
7. Season each fillet with salt and pepper to taste.
8. Pour 1 tablespoon of white wine over each fillet.
9. Place a small piece of butter on top of each fillet.
10. Fold the edges of the aluminum foil together to create a sealed packet around each fillet.
11. Place the packets on a baking sheet and bake for 25 minutes.
12. Remove from the oven and let cool for a few minutes before serving.

Nutrition: Each portion of Filetti di Dentice al Cartoccio contains approximately: Calories: 375 Fat: 25 g Carbohydrates: 3 g Protein: 35 g Sodium: 314 mg Cholesterol: 115 mg

FILETTI DI BRANZINO ALLA GENOVESE GENOA-STYLE BRANZINO WITH POTATOES AND OLIVES

Cook Time: 25 minutes

Serving: 4

Ingredients:
- 4 Branzino fillets (6-8 oz each)
- 4 medium potatoes, peeled and cut into thin slices
- 1 cup of green olives, pitted and chopped
- 3 cloves of garlic, minced
- 1/2 cup of extra-virgin olive oil
- 1 lemon, sliced
- Salt and black pepper, to taste

- Fresh parsley, chopped (optional, for garnish)

Preparation:
1. Preheat oven to 400°F.
2. In a large oven-safe dish, spread half of the sliced potatoes evenly on the bottom.
3. Season each Branzino fillet with salt and pepper and place it over the potatoes in the dish.
4. Sprinkle the chopped olives, minced garlic, and lemon slices over the fillets.
5. Cover the fish with the remaining sliced potatoes.
6. Drizzle the olive oil over the top of the dish and season with additional salt and pepper, if needed.
7. Bake in the oven for 20-25 minutes, or until the fish is cooked through and the potatoes are tender.
8. Garnish with chopped parsley, if desired.

Nutrition: (per serving) Calories: 550 Fat: 42g Carbohydrates: 31g Protein: 25g Sodium: 880mg

POLPETTE AL TONNO TUNA MEATBALLS

Cook time: 25 minutes
Serving: 4 people
Ingredients:
- 1 can of tuna, drained and flaked
- 1 cup of breadcrumbs
- 1/2 cup of grated Parmesan cheese
- 1/2 cup of chopped parsley
- 2 cloves of minced garlic
- 2 large eggs
- Salt and pepper, to taste
- Olive oil, for frying

Preparation:
1. In a large bowl, combine the tuna, breadcrumbs, Parmesan cheese, parsley, garlic, eggs, salt, and pepper.
2. Mix everything together until well combined.
3. Shape the mixture into small balls, about 2-3 cm in diameter.
4. Heat a large frying pan over medium heat with some olive oil.
5. Place the tuna balls in the pan and cook for about 12-15 minutes, until they are golden brown and cooked through.
6. Serve the tuna meatballs hot with some dipping sauce, such as tomato ketchup or mayonnaise.

Nutrition (per serving): Calories: 334 Fat: 15 g Protein: 26 g Carbs: 20 g Fiber: 2 g Sugar: 2 g Sodium: 485 mg

SALMONE CON FINOCCHIO BAKED SALMON FILLETS WITH SHAVED FENNEL

Cook time: 25 minutes
Serving: 4
Ingredients:
- 4 salmon fillets (6 ounces each)
- 1 medium fennel bulb, thinly sliced
- 1 lemon, thinly sliced
- 2 tablespoons olive oil

- 1 teaspoon salt
- 1 teaspoon black pepper
- 2 tablespoons chopped fresh parsley

Preparation:
1. Preheat oven to 400°F.
2. Line a large baking dish with parchment paper or aluminum foil.
3. Arrange the salmon fillets in the dish.
4. Top each fillet with a layer of fennel slices.
5. Place a lemon slice on top of each fennel layer.
6. Drizzle olive oil over the salmon and fennel.
7. Sprinkle salt and pepper over the top.
8. Bake for 25 minutes, or until the salmon is cooked through.
9. Sprinkle with chopped parsley before serving.

Nutrition (per serving): Calories: 327 Fat: 22g Protein: 33g Carbohydrates: 7g Fiber: 2g Sugar: 2g Sodium: 931mg

GAMBERONI ALLA BUSARA VENETIAN-STYLE PRAWNS IN TOMATO SAUCE

Cook time: 30 minutes
Serving: 4
Ingredients:
- 1 kilogram of prawns, peeled and deveined
- 4 garlic cloves, minced
- 2 red onions, diced
- 1 can of chopped tomatoes
- 1 tablespoon of tomato paste
- 1/4 cup of white wine
- 1 teaspoon of dried oregano
- Salt and pepper to taste
- Olive oil
- Fresh parsley leaves for garnish

Preparation:
1. In a large pan, heat 2 tablespoons of olive oil over medium heat.
2. Add the diced onions and cook until soft, about 5 minutes.
3. Add the minced garlic and cook for another minute.
4. Add the canned tomatoes, tomato paste, white wine, oregano, salt, and pepper. Stir everything together and let the sauce simmer for 10 minutes.
5. Add the prawns to the pan and cook for 5-7 minutes or until they are pink and cooked through.
6. Serve the prawns in bowls and garnish with fresh parsley leaves.

Nutrition (per serving): Calories: 365 Fat: 18 g Protein: 38 g Carbohydrates: 20 g Fiber: 3 g Sugar: 11 g

VEGETABLES

PARMIGIANA DI MELANZANE EGGPLANT PARMIGIANA

Cook Time: 1 hour
Serving: 6
Ingredients:
- 4 medium eggplants
- 2 cups of tomato sauce
- 1 cup of all-purpose flour
- 2 eggs
- 2 cups of breadcrumbs
- 1 cup of grated parmesan cheese
- 1 cup of mozzarella cheese
- Salt and pepper to taste
- Olive oil for frying

Preparation:
1. Slice the eggplants into 1/2 inch rounds and sprinkle them with salt. Leave them to sit for 30 minutes to release the excess moisture.
2. Rinse the eggplant slices and pat them dry with a paper towel.
3. In a shallow dish, whisk together the flour and eggs.
4. In another shallow dish, mix together the breadcrumbs and parmesan cheese.
5. Coat each eggplant slice in the flour mixture, then in the egg mixture, and finally in the breadcrumb mixture.
6. Heat the olive oil in a large skillet over medium heat. Fry the eggplant slices until golden brown on both sides, about 4 minutes per side.
7. Preheat the oven to 375°F (190°C).
8. In a 9x13 inch baking dish, spread 1 cup of tomato sauce on the bottom.
9. Layer half of the eggplant slices on top of the sauce, then sprinkle with mozzarella cheese. Repeat with the remaining eggplant slices, sauce, and cheese.
10. Bake for 30 minutes, or until the cheese is melted and bubbly.

Nutrition: (per serving) Calories: 422 Fat: 23.5g Saturated Fat: 9.5g Cholesterol: 108mg Sodium: 649mg Carbohydrates: 33.5g Fiber: 8.3g Sugar: 14.6g Protein: 21g

CAPONATA DI MELANZANE SICILIAN EGGPLANT STEW

Cook time: 30 minutes
Serving: 4 people
Ingredients:
- 3 medium eggplants, diced
- 1 red onion, chopped
- 4 garlic cloves, minced
- 2 tablespoons olive oil
- 1 cup of diced tomatoes
- 1/2 cup of green olives, sliced
- 2 tablespoons of capers
- 2 tablespoons of sugar

- 2 tablespoons of red wine vinegar
- Salt and pepper, to taste
- Fresh basil leaves, chopped, for garnish

Preparation:
1. In a large skillet, heat the olive oil over medium heat.
2. Add the eggplant, onion, and garlic and cook until the eggplant is soft and lightly browned, about 10 minutes.
3. Stir in the tomatoes, olives, capers, sugar, red wine vinegar, salt, and pepper.
4. Simmer the stew until the flavors are well combined, about 15 minutes.
5. Serve hot, garnished with fresh basil leaves.

Nutrition (per serving): Calories: 168 Fat: 12g Protein: 2g Carbohydrates: 15g Sodium: 773mg Fiber: 4g

POMODORI GRATINATI BAKED TOMATO GRATIN

Cook time: 25-30 minutes
Serving: 4-6
Ingredients:
- 6 medium sized tomatoes
- 2 cloves of garlic, minced
- 2 tbsp olive oil
- 1 cup breadcrumbs
- 1/4 cup grated Parmesan cheese
- 2 tbsp fresh basil, chopped
- Salt and pepper to taste

Preparation:
1. Preheat oven to 400°F (200°C).
2. Slice the tomatoes and place them in a baking dish.
3. In a small bowl, mix together the minced garlic, olive oil, breadcrumbs, Parmesan cheese, fresh basil, salt, and pepper.
4. Sprinkle the breadcrumb mixture evenly over the sliced tomatoes.
5. Bake in the oven for 25-30 minutes or until the breadcrumbs are golden brown and the tomatoes are tender.
6. Serve hot.

Nutrition: Serving size: 1/6 of the dish Calories: 140 Fat: 9g Protein: 6g Carbohydrates: 11g Sodium: 300mg Fiber: 2g.

POMODORI RIPIENI TOMATOES STUFFED WITH RICE

Cook time: 45 minutes
Serving: 4-6 people
Ingredients:
- 4 medium-sized tomatoes
- 1 cup of uncooked white rice
- 1 small onion, finely chopped
- 1 clove of garlic, minced
- 1 tbsp of olive oil
- 1 tsp of dried basil

- Salt and pepper, to taste
- 1 cup of chicken or vegetable broth
- 1 cup of grated Parmesan cheese

Preparation:
1. Preheat the oven to 400°F (200°C).
2. Cut the tops off the tomatoes and scoop out the seeds and flesh using a spoon.
3. In a pan, heat the olive oil and sauté the onion and garlic until the onion is translucent.
4. Add the rice and cook for 2-3 minutes, stirring occasionally, until the rice is evenly coated with oil.
5. Add the broth, dried basil, salt, and pepper to the pan and bring the mixture to a boil. Reduce heat to low, cover and let cook for 18-20 minutes.
6. Stir in the grated Parmesan cheese.
7. Fill each tomato with the rice mixture and place them in a baking dish.
8. Bake in the oven for 25-30 minutes, or until the tomatoes are tender and the tops are golden.

Nutrition (per serving): Calories: 200 Fat: 8g Carbohydrates: 22g Protein: 9g Fiber: 2g Sodium: 340mg

PEPERONATA SAUTEED PEPPERS

Cook time: 20 minutes
Serving: 4-6
Ingredients:
- 4 large bell peppers, sliced
- 2 tablespoons olive oil
- 1 large onion, sliced
- 2 garlic cloves, minced
- 1 teaspoon dried oregano
- Salt and pepper to taste
- 1 teaspoon balsamic vinegar
- 1 tablespoon chopped fresh basil

Preparation:
1. Heat the olive oil in a large skillet over medium heat.
2. Add the sliced onion and cook until it is soft and translucent, about 5 minutes.
3. Add the sliced bell peppers and cook for another 5 minutes until they are tender.
4. Stir in the minced garlic and dried oregano. Cook for an additional minute.
5. Season with salt and pepper to taste.
6. Stir in the balsamic vinegar and cook for another minute.
7. Remove from heat and sprinkle with chopped basil before serving.

Nutrition (per serving): Calories: 106 Fat: 9 g Sodium: 140 mg Carbohydrates: 8 g Protein: 1 g

FAGIOLINI ALLA GENOVESE GENOA-STYLE GREEN BEANS

Cook Time: 20 minutes
Serving: 4 people
Ingredients:
- 1 lb. green beans, trimmed
- 1 onion, chopped
- 3 garlic cloves, minced
- 2 tablespoons olive oil

- 1/2 cup chicken broth
- 1/2 cup canned diced tomatoes
- 2 tablespoons chopped fresh basil
- Salt and pepper to taste

Preparation:
1. In a large saucepan, heat the olive oil over medium heat. Add the onion and garlic and cook until soft, about 5 minutes.
2. Add the green beans to the pan and stir to combine with the onion and garlic. Cook for an additional 5 minutes.
3. Pour in the chicken broth and diced tomatoes, stirring well.
4. Bring the mixture to a boil, then reduce heat and simmer for 10 minutes, or until the green beans are tender.
5. Stir in the basil and season with salt and pepper to taste.

Nutrition: (per serving) Calories: 105 Fat: 7 g Saturated Fat: 1 g Cholesterol: 2 mg Sodium: 295 mg Carbohydrates: 10 g Fiber: 4 g Sugar: 4 g Protein: 3 g

CARCIOLI ALLA ROMANA ROMAN-STYLE ARTICHOKES

Cook time: 25 minutes
Serving: 4
Ingredients:
- 4 large artichokes
- 2 lemons, juiced
- 1 cup olive oil
- 4 cloves garlic, minced
- 2 teaspoons dried thyme
- Salt and pepper to taste
- 2 cups breadcrumbs
- 1/2 cup freshly grated parmesan cheese

Preparation:
1. Rinse and clean the artichokes by removing the tough outer leaves and trimming the tops. Cut the artichokes in half lengthwise and remove the hairy center and choke.
2. Place the artichokes in a large pot and cover with water. Add lemon juice and simmer until the artichokes are tender, about 15-20 minutes.
3. In a separate pan, heat the olive oil over medium heat. Add garlic and thyme and cook until fragrant, about 2 minutes.
4. In a bowl, mix together breadcrumbs, parmesan cheese, salt, and pepper.
5. Preheat the oven to 375°F.
6. Dip each artichoke half into the olive oil mixture, then coat with the breadcrumb mixture.
7. Place the artichokes in a baking dish and bake for 10-15 minutes, or until golden brown and crispy.

Nutrition: Servings: 4 Serving Size: 1 artichoke half Caloric Content: 320 calories Fat: 26 g Carbohydrates: 21 g Protein: 8 g Sodium: 550 mg Fiber: 6 g

INSALATA CALABRESE DI PATATE CALABRIAN-STYLE POTATO SALAD

Cook time: 30 minutes

Serving: 4-6 people
Ingredients:
- 2 lbs potatoes, peeled and cubed
- 1 red bell pepper, diced
- 1 yellow bell pepper, diced
- 1 red onion, diced
- 1/2 cup black olives, pitted and chopped
- 1/2 cup red wine vinegar
- 1/2 cup extra virgin olive oil
- 2 cloves garlic, minced
- Salt and pepper to taste
- Fresh parsley, chopped for garnish

Preparation:
1. Boil the potatoes in a pot of salted water for 15-20 minutes or until tender. Drain and let cool.
2. In a large bowl, combine the cooled potatoes, bell peppers, onion, and olives.
3. In a separate bowl, whisk together the vinegar, oil, garlic, salt, and pepper.
4. Pour the dressing over the potato mixture and toss to combine.
5. Cover and refrigerate for at least 1 hour before serving.
6. Before serving, sprinkle with chopped parsley for garnish.

Nutrition: Calories: 280 per serving Fat: 21 g Saturated Fat: 3 g Cholesterol: 0 mg Sodium: 324 mg Carbohydrates: 22 g Fiber: 3 g Sugar: 3 g Protein: 4 g

PATATE ARROSTE ROASTED POTATOES

Cook time: 25-30 minutes
Serving: 4
Ingredients:
- 4 medium potatoes
- 2 tbsp olive oil
- 1 tsp salt
- 1 tsp black pepper
- 1 tsp garlic powder
- 1 tsp paprika
- 1 tsp dried thyme

Preparation:
1. Preheat the oven to 200°C.
2. Wash and peel the potatoes, and then cut them into small wedges.
3. In a large bowl, mix the potatoes with the olive oil, salt, pepper, garlic powder, paprika, and thyme.
4. Transfer the potatoes to a baking tray and bake for 25-30 minutes, or until they are crispy and golden brown.
5. Serve hot as a side dish or as a snack.

Nutrition: Per serving (based on 4 servings):Calories: 235 Fat: 13g Carbohydrates: 27g Protein: 4g Fiber: 3g Sodium: 619mg

PASTICCIO DI PATATE CON FUNGHI POTATO LASAGNA WITH MUSHROOMS

Cook time: 45 minutes
Serving: 4-6 people
Ingredients:
- 1 kg of potatoes
- 250 g of mushrooms
- 1 onion
- 2 cloves of garlic
- 2 tablespoons of olive oil
- 1 tablespoon of dried thyme
- 2 tablespoons of flour
- 500 ml of milk
- 100 g of grated parmesan cheese
- Salt and pepper to taste

Preparation:
1. Preheat the oven to 200°C.
2. Peel and slice the potatoes into thin rounds.
3. Finely chop the onion and garlic. Slice the mushrooms.
4. In a large skillet, heat the olive oil and sauté the onion and garlic until softened.
5. Add the sliced mushrooms to the skillet and cook until browned.
6. Add the thyme and flour to the skillet, and stir to combine. Gradually pour in the milk while stirring constantly.
7. Season with salt and pepper to taste, and cook until the mixture has thickened.
8. In a large oven-safe dish, layer half of the sliced potatoes. Spread half of the mushroom mixture over the potatoes. Repeat the layering process, ending with the mushroom mixture on top.
9. Sprinkle the grated parmesan cheese over the top.
10. Bake in the oven for 35-40 minutes, or until the potatoes are tender and the cheese is golden brown.

Nutrition (per serving): Calories: 306 Total Fat: 15 g Saturated Fat: 6 g Cholesterol: 27 mg Sodium: 257 mg Total Carbohydrates: 31 g Dietary Fiber: 4 g Sugar: 5 g Protein: 11 g

DESSERTS AND DRINKS

TIRAMISII

Cook time: 30 minutes
Serving: 6-8 people
Ingredients:
- 6 egg yolks
- 3/4 cup white sugar
- 2/3 cup milk
- 1 1/4 cups heavy whipping cream
- 1/4 teaspoon vanilla extract
- 24 ladyfingers
- 2 tablespoons instant coffee or espresso
- 2 tablespoons rum
- 1/4 cup boiling water
- 2 tablespoons unsweetened cocoa powder

Preparation:
1. In a medium saucepan, whisk together egg yolks and sugar until well blended. Whisk in milk and cook over low heat, stirring constantly, until mixture thickens and coats the back of a spoon. Remove from heat, pour into a bowl, and allow to cool.
2. In a large bowl, beat whipping cream with vanilla extract until thick. Fold the egg mixture into the whipped cream.
3. Dissolve instant coffee and rum in boiling water. Split the ladyfingers in half and arrange half of them in a single layer in a 9x13 inch dish. Drizzle with half of the coffee mixture and spread half of the egg mixture over the ladyfingers. Repeat layering with remaining ladyfingers, coffee mixture, and egg mixture.
4. Cover and chill in the refrigerator for at least 2 hours or overnight. Before serving, sprinkle with cocoa powder.

Nutrition (per serving, based on 8 servings): Calories: 380 Fat: 21 g Saturated Fat: 12 g Cholesterol: 209 mg Sodium: 85 mg Carbohydrates: 39 g Protein: 8 g

PANNA COTTA WITH BERRY SAUCE

Cook time: 20 minutes
Serving: 4-6
Ingredients:
- 1 1/2 cups heavy cream
- 1/2 cup whole milk
- 1/2 cup granulated sugar
- 1 tsp vanilla extract
- 2 tsp unflavored gelatin powder
- 2 tbsp cold water
- 1 1/2 cups mixed berries (strawberries, raspberries, blueberries)
- 2 tbsp granulated sugar
- 1 tsp lemon juice

Preparation:

1. In a medium saucepan, heat the heavy cream, milk, and sugar over medium heat, stirring occasionally, until the sugar has dissolved and the mixture is hot.
2. Remove from heat and stir in the vanilla extract.
3. In a small bowl, sprinkle the gelatin powder over the cold water and let it stand for a few minutes to soften.
4. Add the softened gelatin to the warm cream mixture and stir until dissolved.
5. Pour the mixture into serving glasses and refrigerate for at least 2 hours, or until set.
6. To make the berry sauce, combine the mixed berries, sugar, and lemon juice in a small saucepan over medium heat. Cook until the berries have broken down and the sauce has thickened, about 10 minutes.
7. Serve the panna cotta with the berry sauce on top.

Nutrition (per serving, based on 6 servings): Calories: 251 Fat: 16g Carbohydrates: 26g Protein: 3g

CANTUCCI BISCOTTI

Cook time: 30 minutes
Serving: Makes approximately 24 biscotti
Ingredients:
- 2 cups all-purpose flour
- 1 cup sugar
- 2 teaspoons baking powder
- 3 eggs
- 1 teaspoon vanilla extract
- 1/2 teaspoon almond extract
- 1/2 cup almonds, chopped

Preparation:
1. Preheat oven to 350°F. Line a baking sheet with parchment paper.
2. In a large bowl, mix together the flour, sugar, and baking powder.
3. Add the eggs, vanilla extract, and almond extract to the dry ingredients and mix until well combined.
4. Fold in the chopped almonds.
5. Divide the dough into two equal parts and form each into a log about 2 inches wide and 12 inches long.
6. Place the logs onto the prepared baking sheet and bake for 25-30 minutes, or until the logs are golden brown.
7. Remove the logs from the oven and allow them to cool for 10 minutes.
8. Using a serrated knife, slice the logs into 1/2 inch thick slices.
9. Place the slices back onto the baking sheet and bake for an additional 10 minutes, or until the slices are lightly golden brown.

Nutrition (per biscotti): Calories: 96 Fat: 3g Saturated Fat: 0.5g Cholesterol: 22mg Sodium: 15mg Carbohydrates: 16g Fiber: 1g Sugar: 8g Protein: 2g.

PASTICCINI ALLE MANDORLE ALMOND COOKIES

Cook time: 20 minutes
Serving: Makes about 20 cookies
Ingredients:

- 1 cup of almonds, finely ground
- 1 cup of all-purpose flour
- 1/2 cup of unsalted butter, at room temperature
- 1/2 cup of granulated sugar
- 1 egg
- 1 tsp of vanilla extract
- Pinch of salt

Preparation:
1. Preheat the oven to 350°F (180°C). Line a baking sheet with parchment paper.
2. In a bowl, beat together the butter and sugar until light and fluffy, about 2-3 minutes.
3. Beat in the egg, followed by the vanilla extract.
4. In a separate bowl, whisk together the flour, ground almonds and salt.
5. Gradually add the dry ingredients to the butter mixture and mix until just combined.
6. Roll the dough into small balls, about 1 inch in size, and place them on the prepared baking sheet.
7. Use the bottom of a glass to gently press down on each ball to flatten it slightly.
8. Bake for about 20 minutes or until the edges are golden brown.
9. Remove from the oven and let cool on the baking sheet for 5 minutes before transferring to a wire rack to cool completely.

Nutrition: (per cookie) Calories: 95 Fat: 7g Saturated Fat: 3g Carbohydrates: 8g Protein: 2g Sugar: 5g Sodium: 6mg

ZEPPOLE ALLA RICOTTA RICOTTA FRITTERS

Cook time: 20 minutes
Serving: 6-8
Ingredients:
- 2 cups of all-purpose flour
- 2 teaspoons of baking powder
- 1/2 teaspoon of salt
- 1/2 cup of sugar
- 2 eggs
- 1/2 cup of whole milk
- 1/2 cup of ricotta cheese
- 1/2 teaspoon of vanilla extract
- Vegetable oil for frying

Preparation:
1. In a large bowl, mix together the flour, baking powder, and salt.
2. In a separate bowl, beat the eggs, sugar, milk, ricotta cheese, and vanilla extract.
3. Add the wet mixture to the dry mixture and stir until well combined.
4. Pour the vegetable oil into a large pot and heat to 375°F (190°C).
5. Use a spoon or a cookie scoop to drop spoonfuls of batter into the hot oil. Fry for 3-4 minutes or until golden brown.
6. Remove with a slotted spoon and drain on paper towels.
7. Serve warm, dusted with powdered sugar.

Nutrition: (per serving) Calories: 183 Total Fat: 10 g Saturated Fat: 4 g Cholesterol: 53 mg Sodium: 176 mg Total Carbohydrates: 20 g Dietary Fiber: 1 g Sugar: 8 g Protein: 5 g.

TORTA DELLA NONNA GRANDMA'S CAKE

Cook time: 35 minutes
Serving: 8
Ingredients:
- 1 1/2 cups all-purpose flour
- 1/2 cup granulated sugar
- 1 tsp baking powder
- 1/4 tsp salt
- 3 eggs
- 1/2 cup unsalted butter, melted
- 1 tsp vanilla extract
- 1/2 cup whole milk
- 1/2 cup grated Parmesan cheese
- 1/4 cup pine nuts
- 2 tbsp lemon zest
- 2 tbsp lemon juice
- powdered sugar for dusting

Preparation:
1. Preheat oven to 375°F (190°C).
2. In a medium bowl, whisk together the flour, sugar, baking powder, and salt.
3. In another bowl, beat the eggs until light and frothy.
4. Add the melted butter, vanilla extract, and whole milk to the eggs and mix well.
5. Slowly add the dry ingredients to the wet ingredients and mix until well combined.
6. Stir in the grated Parmesan cheese, pine nuts, lemon zest, and lemon juice.
7. Pour the batter into a 9-inch (23 cm) round cake pan that has been greased and dusted with flour.
8. Bake for 35 minutes or until a toothpick inserted into the center of the cake comes out clean.
9. Let the cake cool for 10 minutes in the pan, then transfer it to a wire rack to cool completely.
10. Dust the top of the cake with powdered sugar before serving.

Nutrition: Per serving (based on 8 servings): Calories: 365 Fat: 26 g Saturated Fat: 14 g Cholesterol: 147 mg Sodium: 239 mg Carbohydrates: 27 g Fiber: 1 g Sugar: 15 g Protein: 8 g

BACI DI DAMA CHOCOLATE AND HAZELNUT SANDWICH COOKIES

Cook time: 25 minutes
Serving: Makes about 20 cookies
Ingredients:
- 2 cups all-purpose flour
- 1/2 cup unsweetened cocoa powder
- 1/2 teaspoon baking powder
- 1/2 teaspoon salt
- 1/2 cup unsalted butter, room temperature
- 1/2 cup granulated sugar
- 1 large egg
- 1 teaspoon vanilla extract

- 1/2 cup hazelnut spread (such as Nutella)

Preparation:
1. Preheat the oven to 350°F (175°C). Line a baking sheet with parchment paper.
2. In a medium bowl, whisk together the flour, cocoa powder, baking powder, and salt.
3. In a large bowl, beat the butter and sugar together until light and fluffy. Beat in the egg and vanilla extract.
4. Gradually add the dry ingredients to the butter mixture, mixing until just combined.
5. Using a cookie scoop or tablespoon, form the dough into 1-inch balls. Place them 2 inches apart on the prepared baking sheet.
6. Use a fork to press down the center of each cookie to make an indentation. Fill the indentation with a heaping teaspoon of hazelnut spread.
7. Bake for 12-15 minutes, or until the edges are set and the tops are lightly cracked.
8. Cool on the baking sheet for 5 minutes, then transfer to a wire rack to cool completely.

Nutrition: Per cookie (based on 20 servings): about 200 calories, 12g fat, 22g carbohydrates, 2g protein.

MIGLIACCIO NEAPOLITAN RICOTTA CAKE

Cook time: 40 minutes
Serving: 8-10 people
Ingredients:
- 1/2 cup unsalted butter, room temperature
- 1 cup sugar
- 3 eggs
- 1 1/2 cups all-purpose flour
- 1 teaspoon baking powder
- 1/2 teaspoon baking soda
- 1/2 teaspoon salt
- 1 cup ricotta cheese
- 1 teaspoon vanilla extract
- 1/2 cup chopped walnuts (optional)

Preparation:
1. Preheat oven to 350°F (180°C). Grease a 9-inch round cake pan.
2. In a large mixing bowl, cream together butter and sugar until light and fluffy.
3. Beat in eggs one at a time.
4. In a separate bowl, whisk together flour, baking powder, baking soda, and salt.
5. Gradually add the flour mixture to the butter mixture, alternating with the ricotta cheese. Mix until well combined.
6. Stir in the vanilla extract and chopped walnuts, if using.
7. Pour batter into the prepared pan and smooth out the top.
8. Bake for 35-40 minutes or until a toothpick inserted into the center comes out clean.
9. Let the cake cool in the pan for 10 minutes before transferring it to a wire rack to cool completely.

Nutrition (per serving, based on 10 servings): Calories: 333 Fat: 19 g Carbohydrates: 37 g Protein: 8 g Sodium: 259 mg

ROMAN MARITOZZI ALLA PANNA

Cook time: 15 minutes
Serving: 4 servings
Ingredients:
- 8 Roman Maritozzi (Italian sweet buns)
- 2 cups heavy cream
- 1/2 cup granulated sugar
- 1 teaspoon vanilla extract
- 1/4 teaspoon nutmeg (optional)

Preparation:
1. Preheat oven to 375°F (190°C).
2. Cut the Maritozzi in half horizontally and place them in a baking dish.
3. In a saucepan, combine the heavy cream, sugar, vanilla extract, and nutmeg (if using).
4. Heat the mixture over medium heat, stirring occasionally, until the sugar has dissolved and the cream is hot.
5. Pour the cream mixture over the Maritozzi, making sure they are well coated.
6. Bake in the oven for 15 minutes or until the cream is slightly golden and bubbly.
7. Serve hot.

Nutrition (per serving): Calories: 572 Fat: 42g Protein: 8g Carbohydrates: 44g Sugar: 29g Sodium: 213mg

CANNONCINI ALLA CREMA CREAM-STUFFED HORNS

Cook time: 30 minutes
Serving: 4
Ingredients:
- 8 cannoncini (horn-shaped pastries)
- 1 cup heavy cream
- 1/2 cup powdered sugar
- 1 tsp vanilla extract
- Cocoa powder (for dusting)

Preparation:
1. Preheat oven to 400°F (200°C).
2. Cut off the tops of the cannoncini and set aside.
3. In a medium bowl, whip the heavy cream until soft peaks form.
4. Add in the powdered sugar and vanilla extract, and continue whipping until the mixture forms stiff peaks.
5. Fill each cannoncino with the whipped cream mixture.
6. Replace the cut-off tops on the cannoncini.
7. Bake in the preheated oven for 12-15 minutes, or until the cannoncini are golden brown.
8. Dust with cocoa powder before serving.

Nutrition: Per serving (2 cannoncini): Calories: 280 Fat: 26g Carbohydrates: 15g Protein: 2g

SPRITZ COCKTAIL

Cook time: 5 minutes
Serving: 1
Ingredients:
- Prosecco

- Aperol
- Club soda
- Orange wedge (optional garnish)

Preparation:
1. Fill a wine glass with ice.
2. Pour equal parts Prosecco and Aperol over the ice.
3. Top off the drink with club soda.
4. Stir gently.
5. Garnish with an orange wedge, if desired.

Nutrition: Per serving: Calories: 165 Total Fat: 0g Saturated Fat: 0g Cholesterol: 0mg Sodium: 9mg Total Carbohydrates: 15g Dietary Fiber: 0g Sugar: 15g Protein: 0g.

BELLINI COCKTAIL

Cook time: 2 minutes
Serving: 1 serving
Ingredients:
- 1 oz Prosecco
- 1 oz Peach Nectar
- 1 oz White Peach Puree

Preparation:
1. Fill a cocktail shaker with ice.
2. Add Prosecco, Peach Nectar, and White Peach Puree.
3. Shake well.
4. Pour into a chilled champagne glass.
5. Serve immediately.

Nutrition (per serving): Calories: 150 Fat: 0g Saturated Fat: 0g Carbohydrates: 19g Sugar: 17g Protein: 1g

MIMOSA COCKTAIL

Cook time: 5 minutes
Serving: 1 drink
Ingredients:
- 1 oz fresh squeezed orange juice
- 1 oz champagne
- 1 oz triple sec
- splash of grenadine
- orange wedge for garnish

Preparation:
1. Fill a glass with ice.
2. Pour in the orange juice, champagne, and triple sec.
3. Add a splash of grenadine for a pop of color and sweetness.
4. Stir gently.
5. Garnish with an orange wedge and enjoy!

Nutrition: Serving size: 1 drink Calories: 150 Fat: 0g Carbohydrates: 12g Protein: 1g Sodium: 10mg

SGROPPINO COCKTAIL

Cook time: 5 minutes
Serving: 1
Ingredients:
- 1 scoop lemon sorbet
- 1 oz vodka
- 1 oz prosecco
- 1 oz sparkling water
- lemon zest for garnish

Preparation:
1. Fill a martini glass with the lemon sorbet.
2. In a mixing glass, combine the vodka and prosecco.
3. Pour the mixture over the sorbet in the martini glass.
4. Add the sparkling water and gently stir.
5. Garnish with lemon zest.
6. Serve immediately and enjoy.

Nutrition: Calories: approximately 150 Fat: 0g Carbohydrates: 14g Protein: 1g

CONCLUSION

Thank you for joining me on this culinary journey through the rich and diverse world of Italian cuisine. From simple pasta dishes to complex sauces and desserts, Italian cooking offers a wealth of delicious and satisfying recipes that are sure to please any palate.

Whether you're a seasoned home cook or just starting out, this Italian cookbook has hopefully provided you with a range of techniques and tips to help you bring the flavors of Italy into your kitchen. Remember, the key to Italian cooking is using high-quality, fresh ingredients and letting their natural flavors shine through.

So, grab your apron and get ready to explore the delicious world of Italian cuisine. Whether you're cooking for your family or hosting a dinner party, there's a wealth of delicious and satisfying recipes to choose from that will have everyone asking for seconds.

If you like my book, please give me a positive review

Made in the USA
Las Vegas, NV
17 July 2023